The Biblical Seminar

THE ISRAELITE WOMAN

By the same author:
Colour Terms in the Old Testament
(*Journal for the Study of the Old Testament Supplement Series*, 21)

Athalya Brenner

THE ISRAELITE WOMAN

SOCIAL ROLE AND LITERARY TYPE IN BIBLICAL NARRATIVE

jst

1985

jsot press

For Shalom (Brenner)
and Judy (Brenner-Hill)

Copyright © 1985 JSOT Press

Published by
JSOT Press
Department of Biblical Studies
The University of Sheffield
Sheffield S10 2TN
England

Printed in Great Britain
by Redwood Burn Ltd.,
Trowbridge, Wiltshire.

British Library Cataloguing in Publication Data

Brenner, Athalya
    The Israelite woman : social role and literary type
    in biblical narrative.—(The Biblical seminar,
    ISSN 0266-4984; 2)
    1. Women in the Bible
    I. Title   II. Series
    220.8'3054   BS680.W7

ISBN 0-905774-83-3

CONTENTS

PART II
LITERARY PARADIGMS OF FEMALE TYPES
AND BEHAVIOUR

ABBREVIATIONS

AB	Anchor Bible
AJSL	*American Journal of Semitic Languages*
BDB	Brown, Driver and Briggs, *Hebrew and English Lexicon*
BJS	Brown Judaic Studies
BTB	*Biblical Theology Bulletin*
CAD	Chicago Assyrian Dictionary
JBL	*Journal of Biblical Literature*
CB	Cambridge Bible
CBQ	*Catholic Biblical Quarterly*
HTR	*Harvard Theological Review*
ICC	International Critical Commentary
IEJ	*Israel Exploration Journal*
JAAR	*Journal of the American Academy of Religion*
JPT	*Journal of Psychology and Theology*
JSOT	*Journal for the Study of the Old Testament*
OTL	Old Testament Library
VT	*Vetus Testamentum*

PREFACE

There are two questions concerning stories about women in the Old Testament (stories in which women play a central or the central role) that—to my mind—are especially intriguing. These are: *i.* Can we define, on the basis of biblical literature, women's position in the socio-political sphere beyond their traditional domestic function? In other words, how have women participated in the social institutions of their time and place, and can we uncover the existence of specifically female institutions which were later forgotten or suppressed? *ii.* Can we trace the development of stereotypes and paradigms which are used, again and again, for the description of women, to the extent that many individual portrayals contain strong elements of literary conventions or clichés?

These two issues are the chief concerns of the present study. Part I deals with women in professions and institutions, be they leaders of the community, queens, wise women, authoresses, prophetesses, magicians, or loose women. Part II traces literary types: the Matriarch, the Temptress, the Foreign Woman, and the Ancestress. The subject matter is Old Testament narratives. We shall begin at the literary level and then work up to the socio-cultural significance of each instance dealt with.

The relevant passages will be analysed individually, then related to other Old Testament passages and the views expressed in them. Old Testament legal material and New Testament views will be used as corroborating evidence (more about that below). The basic assumption is that, in most cases, the material reflects the attitudes of male writers. These attitudes, however, should not be *a priori* defined as biased or hostile: the aim of this study is to examine biblical narratives against the literary and sociological framework of biblical thought and times, not to set standards of correct attitudes for a bygone age. I would like to investigate the concepts of Woman and

Womanhood, the comprehension of the female psyche and of the female's appropriate social status—but not for the purpose of pronouncing any kind of value judgment. As stated above, the ground material for this study is Old Testament narrative, not the Law. I feel that the choice should be explained. The social status of women is indeed regulated and reflected by the Law collections of the Torah. However, one cannot always separate utopia from reality as far as the Law of ancient Israel (and of other ancient societies) is concerned. In order to distinguish between prescriptive directions on the one hand and actual practice on the other, one must resort to the evidence of the more independent and less tendentious sources—the narrative material. To be sure, the narratives themselves reflect certain preconceptions and viewpoints too; nevertheless, these are seldom as unified and as constricting (relatively speaking, of course) as those contained in any given corpus of the Law. Furthermore, various synchronous and diachronous layers of the same legal source, not to mention separate sources, cannot always be differentiated with a satisfactory degree of confidence. These were the considerations which informed the choice of narrative material, and in some cases prophetic sayings, as a base for discussion. Legal passages, if and when they are referred to, fulfil the secondary function of highlighting, supporting, or discarding the evidence of the prose tales.

Themes, symbols and attitudes towards women which first appear in the Old Testament are often taken up in the New Testament. In order to trace the lines of development—the crystallization of certain views concerning the female species through amplification, simplification, adaptation, and even distortion of earlier concepts—we shall refer at times to the Gospels as well as to the Epistles. No treatment of internal New Testament questions of authorship and authenticity will be undertaken; although these problems are extremely important, they are not crucial to our task. Even without delving into the intricacies of New Testament criticism one can profitably compare attitudes towards women expressed in it to their counterparts in the Old Testament.

Finally, some details of a technical nature. Each section refers to a biblical passage or passages as a point of departure. The book, chapter and verses relevant to the section are given in brackets, next to its heading. For reasons of convenience, very few biblical verses are quoted *verbatim**; therefore, it is recommended that the reader consult the biblical passage(s) before approaching its discussion in this study.

*The English translation quoted is usually the New English Bible. The spelling of biblical names follows that of the NEB throughout.

Chapter 1

INTRODUCTION

In ancient Israel, as in many other societies, positions of power in the community belonged to the following categories of people: the elders or 'wise men' of the clan, tribe or locality, who acted as leaders and dispensers of justice; persons of religion—priests, prophets, magicians; poets and orators; and military leaders. Once the monarchy was instituted, the king assumed a supreme position at the top of the social hierarchy, and his immediate relatives and courtiers acquired an enormous measure of influence. The king, of course, aspired to subordinate all categories of social power to his own rule: the story of the conflict between Samuel and Saul, Israel's first king, undoubtedly develops the personal angle, but it also reflects how the institution of kingship strove for centralization of power through the subordination of the religious establishment (1 Samuel 15). Under Solomon, traditional tribal frameworks had to be broken up so that a wider national entity could be formed (1 Kings 4). The struggle for political, cultural and religious supremacy between king and local leader, king and prophet, king and priest continues throughout the First Temple era. Then the monarchy is abolished with the destruction of the First Temple, and from the time of the exile to Babylon onwards, the religious establishment reigns supreme. Priests, teachers of the Torah and of religious precepts, scribes, and prophets are the prime movers in community life; and their role becomes increasingly crucial to the welfare of their society, as well as to the development of Judaism.

Where do women stand, as far as these key positions of power are concerned? Beginning at the top of the social scale, can they become ruling monarchs? Can they function as tribal or local elders? Were there female orators and poets who were recognized as such, and who enjoyed an influential position either on the local or the national level? Women in ancient Israel could not officiate as priests;[1] did they practise other religious vocations, such as prophetic activities or magic? Could they, did they, become military leaders—and judges, in the juridical as well as the military sense of the biblical term 'judge'?

Very few women of biblical times tried to acquire positions of prominence outside their home and immediate family, at least according to available Old Testament sources. Of those who tried, even fewer managed to achieve a degree of public recognition. We shall begin the investigation of these women's histories at the top of the social order, then descend downwards and sideways. Chapter 2 will tell the story of women who attempted to conquer the supreme bastion of Israelite male authority—the monarchy. Chapter 3 deals with the (tribal?) institution of 'wise women', which later became forgotten or obsolete; Chapter 4 with women poets and authors; Chapter 5 with prophetesses; and Chapter 6 with magicians, sorcerers, and witches. At the very bottom of the social scale we shall find women whose vocation is an ancient one—that of prostitution. While they seldom become socially prominent, their status as professionals requires that they be included within this part of the investigation (Chapter 7).

The women we shall consider in these six occupational categories—queens, wise women, authors, prophetesses, magicians, and prostitutes—differ from each other in class, status, and social import. The common denominator that links them together is that they all strike out on their own—out of the family circle and into the male domain of political life. Our task will consist of finding how they fared, and to what extent their attempts to manage on their own turned out to be successes or failures.

PART I

WOMEN, PROFESSIONS AND SOCIAL INSTITUTIONS

Chapter 2

QUEENS

a. *Queen mothers*

Israelite society did not admit—or did not want to admit—that a monarch's wife could either be a queen in her own right or her royal spouse's deputy. The Old Testament does not recognize that a woman can act as a ruling partner or as regent (= temporary caretaker monarch) after the king's death. The only females whom the Bible acknowledges as queens are either foreigners or else Hebrew women residing in a foreign court. Thus Vashti is Ahasuerus's queen (Esther 1.11-12, and elsewhere); she has the title of 'Queen', even though we know nothing of her as a ruling monarch; and her substitute will receive the same title (2.4). Ahasuerus took Esther, 'put a royal crown on her head and made her queen instead of Vashti' (2.18). Esther, together with Mordecai, is commissioned to write letters in the king's name and sign them with his royal seal (8.7). However, this was done on one specific occasion; the king makes all final decisions and Esther, although she acts as an *ad hoc* deputy, is subject to his will like any other citizen. Another queen, a foreigner and unique in that she is not a king's wife, is the Queen of Sheba (1 Kings 10 = 2 Chronicles 9). The relevant passages treat her treat her just as they would any other (male) head of state, with no comment on her sex.

Within Israelite society itself a woman could not enjoy an institutional position of influence in court unless she was the queen mother. Then she might even be granted the title $g^e b\hat{i}r\hat{a}$, 'Lady'. The question is: What official rank, if any, does this title refer to?

The only Israelite woman described as $g^e b\hat{i}r\hat{a}$ was Jezebel (2 Kings 10.13). Two Judahite queen mothers also bear the title. One is Jehoiachin's mother (Jeremiah 29.13, 18—otherwise the 'king's mother', 2 Kings 24.15), who was expelled to Babylon together with her unfortunate son and other members of Jerusalem upper classes in 597 BC. The other 'Lady' is Asa's mother[1] (2 Kings 15.13 = 2 Chronicles 15.16). It seems that the latter Lady had a certain amount of religious freedom: she had the right to indulge in the cultic activity of her choice as long as she did so in private, but not to turn this same cult into an official or semi-official practice. At any rate, Asa could cancel out her status as 'Lady' and phase out the cult she had introduced. It appears, then, that even a queen mother who possesses the title g^e^bîrâ—and not every queen mother does—must take orders from her reigning son if and when her son does occupy the throne. It must be remembered, though, that very few royal women actually became 'ladies'. Even Bathsheba is referred to as 'mother of Solomon' (1 Kings 2.13) and 'the king's mother' (2.19), but nothing else. The polite manner which her son Solomon employs in his dealings with her serves to emphasize the fact that he acts contrary to her request (1 Kings 2). The daughter of Pharaoh, Solomon's wife (1 Kings 3.1), has no political significance apart from that inherent in her noble origin; her only sphere of influence is the personal religious one. She is not the mother of Solomon's heir Rehoboam (who, incidentally, is the son of an Ammonite woman–1 Kings 14.21). Hence, extant biblical information implies that it was highly unusual to confer a formal, institutional position on a king's mother (or wife, see b. below). This was unheard of in both kingdoms, Israel and Judah, at least until the ninth century BC, Asa's and Ahab's era; and even from that time onwards it was done but rarely.

In contradistinction, women of neighbouring Near Eastern states could and did attain a higher degree of political involvement on the royal level. There were queens in Mesopotamia as well as in Egypt,[2] although they were not numerous. Indeed, some sources doubt the legitimacy of these queens' reigns or talk about them disparagingly. However, the negative judgment mostly stems from the views held by later generations; in their own time those queens managed to hold on to their elevated posts. The wives of some kings conducted wide-ranging correspondence which had political as well as personal significance.[3] There is even a biblical text that bears witness to the possible institutional importance of a foreign king's wife, this time an Egyptian one. Hadad the Edomite, who tries to overthrow Solomon, marries an Egyptian woman—sister to the 'Lady' (g^e^bîrâ) Tahpenes, wife of Pharaoh (1 Kings 11.20). Here the Egyptian king's wife is given the title which is reserved elsewhere for a few queen mothers only. Therefore, we would do well to investigate what is implied by the official title g^e^bîrâ. In other words, what were the nature and contents of the g^e^bîrâ institution—an institution which is known from the ninth century BC onwards?

This is particularly important since the only other Old Testament term that might be relevant to our problem, *šēgāl*, which is sometimes translated as 'king's wife' (Psalm 45.10; Nehemiah 2.6; and in biblical Aramaic, Daniel 5.2; 3.23), is not of much help for our purpose. It seems late, although the exact date of Psalm 45 cannot be fixed with any certainty. Also, there is no documentation for the usage of *šēgāl* to denote 'king's wife' or 'mistress' during the First Temple era. Finally, at the most the term does denote 'king's wife, mistress' in the Second Temple era, but never specifically 'queen' or 'queen mother'.

As for Asa's mother, Jezebel, Athaliah (who was her son's adviser— 2 Chronicles 22.3—and later became self-styled queen, although she is not called *gᵉbîrâ*), and Jehoiachin's mother—what do they have in common, apart from their title?

Asa was probably quite young when he ascended the throne, for he ruled for forty-one years after his brother Abijam had been king for three years only (1 Kings 15.2). Jehoiachin, too, came to the throne after his elder brother's death. According to 2 Chronicles 36.9 he was then a minor aged eight; the parallel text (2 Kings 24.8) says he was eighteen. Jezebel was the mother of two kings: Ahaziah, who reigned for two years (1 Kings 22.51), and Jehoram who reigned for eleven years before Jehu killed him (2 Kings 9.22). It is possible that Asa's and Jehoiachin's mothers, whose sons were children when enthroned, ruled for a while as regents on behalf of their sons. Similarly Jezebel, after the demise of her two king sons, stepped in so that she could take care of the dynasty's interests. Her final words to Jehu (2 Kings 9.31) make it abundantly clear that she considers herself the legitimate successor to the crown, while Jehu—to her—is a usurper. Athaliah seizes the opportunity to become the monarch after Jehu has killed her son Ahaziah: the latter managed to reign for one year only (2 Kings 8.26). She, however, does not make do with a transition period of temporary regency but tries to prolong it into a permanent arrangement of queenship (2 Kings 11 = 2 Chronicles 22–23.15). Therefore, it seems that a queen mother does not become a 'Lady' unless circumstances cause a gap in the usual transition of political power from a male monarch to his heir. This kind of governmental void may occur when a king–husband dies while his heir apparent is still young and needs protection; a king–son dies suddenly without having any heirs; or two brother–kings die in quick succession.

The principle of using the queen mother to fill the political gap— an obvious choice in an emergency—operated outside ancient Israel as well. Two examples from ancient Mesopotamia come to mind, although both are slightly later than the Old Testament ones. These refer to two wives/mothers/regents of Assyrian kings, Semiramis and Nitokris.[4] In these as in the biblical cases, at the end of the emergency period the right of government returned to the king–son, who had meanwhile matured, or to the next male heir of the royal line. Then the 'Lady' ceases to be the regent. She retains her title but is subject to the new king's authority, be he her son or somebody else. The possibility of such a formal or semi-formal arrangement explains how Asa could deprive his mother of both title and special privileges when he came of age; since, once established, he possessed the supreme royal authority, he used his power to overrule her and put an end to the religious practices he objected to. Apparently, once the new king attained legal maturity and political support, his mother's role was over: she stepped back into the relatively powerless position of queen mother. Her status was no longer anchored in political necessity or fixed custom, and she was once more—like any other person in the realm—answerable to the king. Her opinions concerning affairs of state could now either be taken into account or ignored, according to the king's goodwill. Perhaps Jezebel, who was familiar with this arrangement, attempted to retain the title and secure an advisory capacity for herself from Jehu (2 Kings 9). Had Jehu granted her that, his new rule would have achieved a semblance of legal support from the previous dynasty. Nonetheless, Jehu refused to do that and, indeed, got rid of her; Jezebel's political power was such that, in order to establish his own government, he had to dispose of her first. Her murder does not make sense unless we recognize that, in addition to her strong personality, she had a very real power base in her capacity as regent.

b. *Jezebel (1 Kings 16–2 Kings 10)*

Unlike any other king's wife or mother in the Old Testament, Jezebel was a real queen, assistant and partner in government to her husband Ahab (and, as contended above, regent after his and his sons' death). Even Athaliah, who managed to rule Judah as sole monarch for years after the death of her husband and son, is not described as queen during her husband's lifetime. Jezebel's deeds during Ahab's reign show that she actually participated in the business of government with her husband's consent—not that the Bible stoops to calling her 'queen'. Since she is such an exception to the general rule, the question must be asked: What were the sources of her power? It is possible, of course, to relate her extraordinary status to her husband's fondness for her—or perhaps to his weakness of character. Or is the answer more complicated? Jezebel[5] is described as a foreign princess from Tyre who habitually gets what she is after. She never suffers moral inhibitions or pangs of conscience: this is emphasized by later Jewish sources as well.[6] She worships the Canaanite god Baal. Hence, she is a bitter and active adversary of Israel's true God, his believers and prophets. The main source of her authority is her husband Ahab, a weak if not altogether negative figure. It is implied that she is aggressive and resourceful, full of political initiative and vigour. And yet, when Jehu buries her after her infamous demise he justifies the burial by referring to her foreign royal origin, not to her position within the Israelite royal house (2 Kings 9.34). Finally, Elijah's curse to her husband (1 Kings 21.24) affects *her* manner of death (2 Kings 10.35), not Ahab's. Nevertheless, it is understood that the curse has been fulfilled, for Jezebel, in death as well as in life, is considered an appendix of her husband's. However, some details of this picture do not fit in: Jezebel is much more than an interfering, amoral wife of a monarch. When she threatens Elijah (1 Kings 19.2), after the latter proves on Mt Carmel that his God and not Baal is the only true god of rain and source of cosmic fertility (1 Kings 18), Elijah runs away at once. Apparently he believes that Jezebel has the ability to carry out her threat. Moreover, she has earlier persecuted God's prophets, perhaps even caused Elijah's first flight (1 Kings 17.2-7). The narrator, who comes from prophetic circles, describes Ahab's attitude towards Yahweh and Yahweh's prophets as much more moderate than his wife's (1 Kings 18.17ff.). For instance, Ahab's meeting with Elijah is far from friendly, but not extremely hostile. Jezebel uses the royal seal when she plans the legal murder of Naboth: nowhere is it stated that the seal was given to her for that purpose only (1 Kings 21.8), or that by using it she exceeded the authority invested in her. The sole Old Testament parallel of awarding such a privilege to a king's wife is that of Esther (Esther 8.7). The latter belongs to a foreign court where, according to the Bible, queenship or the entrusting of royal responsibilities to women is more common than inside Israelite society. Nevertheless, it seems that Jezebel enjoyed an exceptional position within this same society, although biblical writers are loath to admit it.

The Baal prophets eat at Jezebel's table (1 Kings 18.19), not Ahab's—and we cannot suspect either the narrator or the editor of wanting to cleanse the king's reputation by assigning the sin of paganism to his wife alone. Thus we can assume that Jezebel had her own court, and sufficient economic means to maintain it. The queenly manner she adopts on her last encounter with Jehu (2 Kings 9.30-31) shows that, at least in her own mind, her position is legitimate. Jehu in fact admits her royal status, although he attributes it to her origins (2 Kings 9.34). So, if Jezebel is such an awful character, why is she so powerful? And if she is powerful, a queen in reality if not in title, what are the sources of her political, legal and religious authority?

Before we approach these questions we must glance at the complex literary history of the narratives in which Jezebel and Ahab feature, so that we can understand the nature of these narratives. The Jezebel–Ahab stories are set within the Elijah–Elisha cycle (1 Kings 17–2 Kings 9, with its sequel in 2 Kings 10). The central figures of the cycle are obviously those of the two great prophets. Other persons, including personages of the royal family, are mentioned only inasmuch as their actions are related to Elijah or Elisha. The authors are not interested in Jezebel or Ahab for their own sake, but in the way their activities and character illuminate those of the prophets. The literary composition itself, whose bulk can be attributed to prophetic circles (judging by the point of view inherent in them), is nevertheless not homogeneous. It contains miracles and legends alongside reports of Elijah's and Elisha's political involvement.[7] To these prophetic tales and reports an editorial framework of a Deuteronomistic nature has been attached. A characteristic feature of this editorial framework is the recurrent negative evaluation (within the Books of Kings) of Northern kings and their official cult of the Golden Calves, which is regarded as the chief reason for the destruction of the Northern Kingdom in 721 BC.[8] Ahab himself is bitterly accused of these practices, together with other idolatrous activities—the worship of Baal and his consort Asherah (1 Kings 16.29-34). Both the prophetic sources and editorial framework treat Ahab with distaste; however, there are hints in the former that Ahab was not altogether without merit. For instance, he is described as deeply regretting Naboth's murder (1 Kings 21.27). In addition to these two distinct sources of information there is, within the text, a third one—official or semi-official documentation (mainly chs. 20 and 22) about Ahab, his royal house and activities. The stories of the last type are balanced and even sympathetic towards Ahab; their judgment of him is much more realistic and positive than that of the other two sources.

The prophetic narratives establish the opinion—which the editorial passages re-inforce—that one of Ahab's greatest sins was his subordination to Jezebel's views and beliefs (1 Kings 16.31-34; 21.25). Although, especially according to the third source, he did perform his administrative and military roles adequately, he is presented as unable or unwilling to curb his wife's criminal deeds. Thus the message of the biblical story is clear: he is the direct cause for the fall of his dynasty. Does this portrait of Ahab make sense? Should we conclude that Ahab was a spineless lover who, like Samson, let his love override all other considerations until it led him to his doom? Had our story been a folk tale, this kind of reasoning would have been acceptable; unfortunately, this is hardly the case. The composite narrative does contain elements of folklore, especially in the miracle reports, but this is only one element of the total composition. Besides, if Ahab were so weak, his weakness—like Samson's—would be all-encompassing. In fact, he did not let Jezebel interfere in all matters of state. Her activities were limited to internal affairs; international and military matters were outside her sphere of influence. It seems, therefore, that we must look elsewhere for the appropriate answer, and ask: What were Jezebel's power bases as queen during her husband's lifetime, and later as regent?

Jezebel was a foreign princess by birth, the daughter of King Ethbaal of Sidon and Tyre (1 Kings 16.31). Josephus writes that this same Ethbaal was priest to the great goddess Ashtoreth (named as a typical Sidonian-Phoenician goddess in 1 Kings 11.5), and that he usurped the throne from a family whose sons were linked to the cult of the same goddess too.[9] The practice of appointing a chief male priest for a goddess's temple, and a chief priestess for a god's temple, is known already in Mesopotamia of the third millennium BC. This custom is highly suitable for fertility cults, for a basic requirement of such a cult is the assurance of continuous fertility on earth and in society, which is symbolized by a dramatization of divine marriage. The dramatized fertility principle was enacted as an annually recurrent sexual union between a local king and the Great Goddess (whatever her local name might be); a king-substitute and the Goddess; a hierodule of either sex and a commoner; or a priest and priestess, direct representatives of the gods they serve. Within such a religious framework, a priestly appointment for the king and an additional female member of the royal household can link the priesthood and the royal family and prove to be a strong cohesive element for governmental stability. The great Akkadian king Sargon (24th–23rd century BC) exploited this politically clever idea to the full. On the one hand, he claimed that in his youth he enjoyed the love of the goddess Ishtar (represented by a priestess of hers?); considered himself a life-long protégé of the same goddess; and, perhaps, was born to a priestess. On the other hand, he strengthened his combined secular-religious rule by appointing his daughter Enheduanna as chief priestess to the moon god at the city of Ur, and to the heaven god at Uruk. From then on, the Mesopotamian custom of appointing one of the reigning king's daughters to the office of chief priestess continued—irrespective of dynastic changes—for hundreds of years.[10]

According to Herodotus, Tyre, the Phoenicians' chief city, was founded already at the beginning of the third millennium.[11] Even if we disregard this Tyrian tradition adopted by Herodotus as unfounded, there is no better evidence for the beginnings of the Phoenician city state: its origin is shrouded in myth. If the Tyrians did come from Mesopotamia, as is widely believed, they probably imported traditional social institutions into their new land. Thus, when they arrived at Tyre they carried with them the custom of appointing a daughter of the reigning king as high priestess for the chief local god, Baal Melqart,[12] who was later identified with the god Heracles. In the case of Jezebel's father Ethbaal this custom gave the royal family an unprecedented advantage: when the king is high priest of Ashtoreth and his daughter is high priestess of Baal they can exercise, between the two of them, a political, economic, and religious monopoly over the whole realm. It follows that, if Jezebel was a Baal priestess from youth, her active fanaticism and special status at her husband's court are self-explanatory. This also explains why Jezebel alone—out of all the prominent foreign women in Israelite and Judaean courts— managed to achieve such an elevated position. Even Pharaoh's daughter, King Solomon's wife, does not come close to Jezebel in importance, influence or authority, although the political alliance she represents is of great significance. Hence, the legal basis for Jezebel's activities and queenly status may not simply have been her foreign royal origin—much made of in the biblical narratives—but rather her office as high priestess and patroness of the Baal cult. Furthermore, a high priestess designate must be educated from birth to govern, for the office requires political expertise and the ability to cooperate with the secular branch of government. Such a woman could prove to be a natural active partner for any king. There was no reason to waste her talents by assigning to her, once married, the merely ornamental role of the king's spouse. And indeed, the Old Testament does not conceal Jezebel's political prowess and legal knowledge (cf. the story of Naboth, 1 Kings 21), although these are presented in a pejorative manner.

Since Baal worship was an important source of Jezebel's authority, her insight dictated the reinforcement of the cult which had enjoyed a popular appeal in Israel even before her time. Therefore she turned it into an official cult which effectively bound the populace to the feminine aspect of the monarchy, inasmuch as Ahab's royal authority was derived from the cult of Yahweh. Because such a doubly strong legitimation of the monarchy suited Ahab's interests, he had no reason for protest. Since he is represented as a liberally minded and realistic statesman—thus at least in the sources that are not directly hostile towards him—he let his wife administer internal affairs on her own. Rational political considerations of this type seem much more in keeping with his thinking than the Samson-like motif of masculine weakness for corrupt feminine wiles.

If we read the text carefully we find that Ahab's overall description is that of a religiously tolerant ruler. The two passages which directly accuse him of participating in—and not only authorizing—his wife's cults of Baal and his consort (1 Kings 16.31-33; 21.25-26) are editorial passages, Deuteronomistic in language and outlook (see above). Otherwise he is presented differently. For instance, no biblical text accuses him of persecuting Yahweh's prophets: he treats the prophets with tolerance (1 Kings 18.16; 20.29), listens to their words (21.27), consults with them before going to war, and keeps them in his court (1 Kings 22). The names of his sons contain the Israelite theophoric elements '-yahu', not '-baal'. His tolerance of both mutually exclusive religions has, apparently, one end in mind: to strengthen his reign from all possible aspects. If he supports the co-existence of his wife's cult together with his own he does that for pragmatic rather than religious considerations. Finally, it seems that he left the religious aspect of internal government to Jezebel, whose education and capabilities made her equal to the role. In a political climate of increasing military pressure from the Aramaeans and

Assyrians, he could do no better than to delegate some authority concerning internal state affairs to his queen–wife.

At this point we must ask: Why, if Jezebel was a high priestess of Baal, do the biblical narratives ignore such an important piece of information? The answer to this question can only be guessed at. The claim that a woman can act in a priestly capacity—especially a foreign woman who worships a foreign god—was probably considered by those who wrote down our stories, and those who later edited them, as bizarre and ridiculous. Within the patriarchal structure of Israelite/Judaean society this kind of appointment had no validity whatsoever. Since the narrators did not admit the validity of female priesthood they could not, perhaps would not, divulge information concerning its existence. At any rate, even though the stories were not constructed primarily to report historical information, they still contain hints which support our hypothesis.

Jezebel, Ahab's chief wife, had probably not only her own compound within the royal court but also an independent administrative organization. This organization was financed by her and answerable to the queen alone. She undoubtedly did as she pleased with her personal fortune, which was considerable. Otherwise, feeding and keeping four hundred and fifty Baal prophets and four hundred Asherah prophets (1 Kings 18.19) would have used up a sizeable part of her religious revenues. Even if the numbers are exaggerated or formulaic—later on we hear that Ahab too had four hundred prophets, albeit Yahweh prophets, in his court (1 Kings 22.6)—they convey the idea that the queen patronized the whole cult organization and controlled it. In her capacity as priestess and patroness she could administer the expenditure and income of Baal's central shrine in Samaria as well as temples at other localities. Regular sources of income such as tithes, vow-money, firstborn offerings, levies, voluntary contributions, and taxes made her into a person of considerable economic strength. She persecuted Yahweh's prophets almost to the point of total extermination (1 Kings 18.4, 13); it follows that she possessed the authority and means to carry out her wishes. Therefore Elijah himself escaped from her without delay (1 Kings 19.2-3). The prophet's fear, and the story of Naboth, prove that her influence encompassed both the political and religious spheres. Her extraordinary power was ultimately derived from her economic independence, while other factors (her origins, personality, office, and husband's esteem) contributed to its magnitude too.

It is Jezebel who initiated Naboth's legal murder. The man's refusal to hand over his ancestral land to the king offended her conception of monarchic rights, as these were exercised in her own homeland. The conflict here is between the Israelite idea of ancestral ownership—with the land conceived of as ultimately belonging to God—over against the Canaanite concept of the king as the feudal landlord of his realm. According to the biblical text Jezebel authorized her command to put Naboth to trial and execute him by using Ahab's name and personal seal (1 Kings 21.8). If indeed she used Ahab's name and authority, why does the report which states that the command has been performed come back to her, not directly to the king (vv. 14-15)? This makes sense only if we understand 'in Ahab's name' to mean 'with his consent'—not because she has let him know beforehand the details of her plan and obtained his permission, but because she usually acted as his representative–signatory for administrative and internal affairs. Nowhere is it said that Ahab handed over his royal seal on this particular occasion and for this specific purpose. Hence, it is likely that Jezebel sealed the letter containing Naboth's fate by using her own seal, which was the symbol of the permanent institutional responsibility Ahab delegated to her.

Prominent women did have their own seals. Seals that belonged to ladies of consequence have been found in Mesopotamia and Egypt. As for our queen, Avigad has found a seal inscribed *Jzbl*. He dates this seal, on palaeographic grounds, to the ninth or eighth century BC.[13] If this is indeed queen Jezebel's seal, then our assumption becomes less tentative. It would follow that the sight of her seal, and the knowledge that it symbolized the authority the king invested in it, made any order of hers legally and officially binding.

What can be learnt about Jezebel's power and status from the curse which follows the Naboth story (1 Kings 21.21-24) and the sorry end of Ahab's dynasty (2 Kings 9–10)?

Elijah's curse concerns Ahab's family, but does not refer explicitly to the king himself (1 Kings 21.21). Neither does the shameful fate prophesied for Jezebel and the rest of the family (vv. 23-24) concern his own person. It seems that the curse, although delivered to Ahab in his capacity as responsible head of the royal house, was primarily directed at the queen and her sons. Ahab himself dies honourably in battle (1 Kings 22.34 onwards) and is buried in the family vault in Samaria (vv. 37-40). It is said that the dogs licked his blood; this, however, looks like an unnecessary attempt at harmonizing events with the text of the curse. The dynasty is hardly in danger at this point, for two sons of Ahab and Jezebel reign before the royal house ceases to exist. The narrator makes it clear that, unlike Jehu's killing of Ahab's sons by other wives (2 Kings 10), the killing of Jezebel and her reigning son Jehoram were expedient. The end of the officially recognized Baal cult in Israel could be achieved only when the queen, together with the king–son she educated in her spirit, were disposed of. In other words, Jehu could not establish the reform he initiated until he got rid of Jezebel. So, the Yahweh–Baal conflict is, in fact, not the story of Elijah versus Ahab or Jehu versus Jehoram, but of Jezebel versus Elijah and Jezebel versus Jehu. Only after the death of the princess/priestess/queen/queen-mother/regent, grand patroness of the Baal cult and prophets, can Jehu abolish the foreign worship (2 Kings 10.18ff.).

To conclude: Jezebel possessed a well-defined personal mandate: she was a partner in her husband's reign. From the outset, her status was derived partly from the king's delegation of governmental responsibilities to her, partly from her own personal authority. Some clues in the Old Testament text, together with supporting evidence from elsewhere, hint that her religio-political power was anchored in Phoenician custom and was re-affirmed by Ahab after they became married. The composite biblical narrative passes an entirely negative judgment on the foreign princess as an immoral usurper of power. The narrators were consistent in their attempts to minimize, even suppress, her important and well-established roles.[14]

c. *Athaliah (2 Kings 11 = 2 Chronicles 22–23.15)*

Athaliah came to Judah from the Northern kingdom. It is not clear whether she was Ahab's sister (2 Kings 8.26; 2 Chronicles 22.2) or his daughter, perhaps by Jezebel (2 Kings 8.18). It seems, though, that 'She was educated under the supervision of queen Jezebel and so influenced by that Tyrian princess. This makes plausible the character of Athaliah and her leanings to the Tyrian worship, which she witnessed daily in Samaria and later tried to introduce to Jerusalem.'[15]

Athaliah married Joram son of Jehoshaphat, the Judaean king who was Ahab's ally. The marriage undoubtedly served to cement the political alliance between the twin states, and to enhance the cultural influence of the North in Judah.

We have no significant details about Athaliah's status and activities during her husband's lifetime. Might we surmise that her position was no different from that of any other king's chief wife? The situation changes when her son Ahaziah comes to the throne, for then she becomes her son's counsellor (2 Chronicles 22.3). The biblical text is phrased thus: 'He (i.e. Ahaziah) too followed the practices of the house of Ahab, for his mother was his counsellor in wickedness'. Although the words are emotionally loaded—they convey the writer's hatred of the queen-mother—they are not very informative. Was Athaliah an unofficial adviser whose opinion carried weight with her son, or did she actually have executive powers? Was her position confirmed legally, or did it depend entirely on her son's good will? Had she carried the title $g^e b \hat{\imath} r \hat{a}$, 'Lady', we might have understood the political meaning of her role better. As it is, we are faced with a problem: when her son died after a short reign of a single year, Athaliah became self-styled queen. She could not have achieved that position without enjoying some measure of political and military support. She therefore must have held a fairly strong position during her son's lifetime, a position which entailed not only the right to advise but also the ability to exercise royal authority.

When Ahaziah died, his 'house . . . had no one strong enough to rule' (2 Chronicles 22.9). Athaliah quickly stepped into the gap, perhaps—at least initially—as an acting regent for the royal house. The narrator strongly condemns her for this unprecedented behaviour. The text grimly states that she killed all scions of royal blood in order to sustain her rule (2 Kings 11.1; the parallel text in 2 Chronicles 22.10 is slightly different). The execution of relatives was not uncommon in the case of newly ordained monarchs who wanted to secure their rule, especially when circumstances were difficult; thus king Solomon kills his half-brother Adonijah (1 Kings 2.13-25). The narrator goes to great pains to justify the act. Joram, Athaliah's husband, killed 'all his brothers' when he became king (2 Chronicles 21.4; but this information does not appear in the parallel passage, 1 Kings 8). Athaliah's cruel actions were probably necessary, particularly because no direct adult male heir existed. Nevertheless, because she was a woman and a foreigner who presumed to occupy the Davidic throne, she does not receive the lenient treatment accorded to Solomon who, after all, had behaved similarly.

Still, Athaliah persevered for over six years, despite the objections of the religious establishment, and possibly the hostility of at least part of the political establishment. This suggests that she was clever and tough. Characteristically, there is almost no information concerning her reign: the text will simply have us believe that she was extremely unpopular. However, if she did survive for a while it must have been because she could control the means to sustain her regime. Her tours of duty as her son's adviser and, later, emergency regent probably helped to form a power base. In addition, she had religious influence too. Like Jezebel—her sister-in-law, mother or step-mother— she introduced the Baal cult into her realm. The existence of a Baal temple in Jerusalem (2 Kings 11.18 = 2 Chronicles 23.17) means that she proclaimed the foreign cult as official, alongside Yahweh's worship, and acted as its patroness. Revenues and power were now hers. Considering the opposition she must have encountered—a foreigner and the first female monarch in the history of Judah—her rule, as long as it lasted, was quite sound.

Her downfall was planned and executed by the Yahwistic priestly circles. The Temple priests were enraged by Athaliah's illegitimate usurpation of the throne (as it seemed to them), and by the official status of the Baal cult. They fought the outrage by orchestrating a carefully organized, almost bloodless *coup d'état* within the Temple grounds. This means that Athaliah was brave enough to come into the Temple complex by herself, a transgression which made the insult of her reign even greater. The *coup* was centred round the minor Joash, who had been smuggled out of court at the time of Athaliah's ascendancy to the throne by his nanny, the priest Jehoiada's wife. The moving spirit and organizer of the conspiracy was Jehoiada himself. We note that, according to the biblical text, no attempt is made by the priestly establishment to institute a theocracy. The priests restored the monarchy to the real heir of the Davidic dynasty, and acted as regents until he came of age: Athaliah was killed (2 Kings 11.16 = 2 Chronicles 23.14-15) and institutional monarchy reinstated under priestly guidance. It is significant that the only blood spilled was that of the unfortunate queen. She must have had, up to this point, troops who were bound by an oath of loyalty directly to her own person. As nothing but her death was sufficient to make the conspiracy successful, it was necessary to lure her to the Temple and trap her there, away from her bodyguards. She herself perceived immediately what was happening: from her viewpoint this was an unlawful conspiracy and treason (2 Kings 11.14 = 2 Chronicles 23.13), because she considered herself the legitimate queen. Her behaviour implied that, until her downfall, she enjoyed a power base whose components were her royal origins; her previous roles as king's wife, king's mother, intimate adviser to her son Ahaziah and regent after his death; her control of the religious establishment (full control of the Baal cult but insufficient control of Yahweh's); and, like Jezebel, her personal capabilities and education.

To conclude: Athaliah's reign was considered illegitimate by the biblical narrator—and by the priests, her contemporaries and adversaries—for the following reasons: she was a woman; she was a foreigner, not born to the house of David; she was a Baal worshipper and introduced his cult into Judah as an official alternative; and she was judged to be bloody and immoral. Let us remember, however, that she did manage to stay in power for years, despite the religio-political opposition. Her political and organizational skills must have been immense. Still, like Jezebel, she was a passing episode only. No other Judaean or Israelite woman managed to become queen again, as far as we can learn from our sources, until late in the Second Temple era; and this already reaches beyond the scope of this study.

d. *Esther*

Ahasuerus took Esther, 'put a royal crown on her head and made her queen instead of Vashti' (Esther 2.18). But what does her admitted 'queenship' consist of? Together with Mordecai, she is given the right to use the royal seal on one specific occasion (8.7; compare Jezebel earlier), but no more. She has no free access to the king: her coming to him without being summoned is done at great personal peril (4.15–5.2). When Ahasuerus declares that he is prepared to give her anything she wants, 'up to half my kingdom' (5.3), she accepts it for what it is meant to be: a figure of speech born out of exaggerated good manners which is not to be taken seriously. In reality Esther has the title of 'queen' and wears queenly garments (5.1), but has no official rights or obligations apart from being the king's chief wife. In other words, she is not a ruling monarch. She resorts to feminine and sexual charms, wine and merriment in order to make the king change his mind and to trap Haman (chs. 5 and 7); for, apparently, no other means of persuasion is available to her. And finally, it is 'Mordecai the Jew who is second only to King Ahasuerus' (10.3) and who wears royal attire as well (8.15). Curiously, then, Esther is 'queen' in nothing but her title and dress, while Jezebel, to whom the biblical text does not accord the title, displays many signs of wielding real monarchic power.

e. *Summary*

A few queen mothers became regents after the death of their royal husbands and sons, or when the king-designate was a minor at the time of his father's demise. The title that was then accorded to them was *gᵉbîrâ*, 'Lady'. This title was given to Asa's mother, Jezebel, and to Jehoiachin's mother. It has perhaps been suppressed in the case of Athaliah. The 'Lady' acted as regent, i.e. temporary monarch, until a new male heir was ready to occupy the throne. The only Old Testament women who acted as reigning monarchs were Jezebel (in the Northern kingdom) and Athaliah (in Judah). Both were royal foreigners and related in blood and outlook.

Jezebel functioned as queen and Baal priestess during her husband's lifetime and as regent later. She derived her power from her origins, religious position and economic independence, Ahab's delegation of authority, and her own personal talents. She was killed by Jehu so that his new regime could be installed.

Athaliah became her son's adviser, and later possibly functioned as regent after his death. She then occupied the Davidic throne and reigned for over six years. Her foreign religious convictions served her well at first, then were used as one of the reasons for her overthrow by the priestly establishment of Yahweh's Temple. Her death paved the way for the reinstatement of the House of David.

In short: the institution of queenship, although recognized in the Old Testament as valid for foreign lands, was considered unacceptable both in Israel and in Judah. The women whose activities have been discussed are the unfortunate exceptions to this rule.

Chapter 3

WISE WOMEN

a. *The term 'wise' and its applications*

The Hebrew adjective *ḥākām*, 'wise', and the noun derived from it, *ḥokmâ*, 'wisdom', have quite a few applications. A 'wise' person might be one who is 'wise' in the administration of social, political, or economic affairs—like Joseph in Egypt (Genesis 41.33, 39). An adviser or counsellor at the royal court might carry the title *ḥākām* (Isaiah 19.11, 12; Esther 6.13; 2 Chronicles 2.13; and more). The adjective might mean 'shrewd, clever, prudent' (2 Samuel 13.3). It refers to the quality of *ḥokmâ*, in the sense of 'skill in technical work' (Isaiah 3.3).

Most occurrences of *ḥākām*, its plural form *ḥᵃkāmîm* and *ḥokmâ*, 'wisdom' appear within biblical Wisdom literature (Proverbs, Ecclesiastes, Job) or in passages that are ideologically related to this literature. Here the usages mentioned above are quite common. However, the Hebrew words signify, more often than not, a class of professional sages who were teachers of religion and ethics. *Ḥākām* in Wisdom literature is, in fact, a generic term which refers to an institution of educators and teachers who deal with theoretical as well as practical knowledge.

Two of the denotations of 'wise' (and its derived terms) refer, then, to social institutions—advisers to kings and statesmen, and teachers of 'wisdom' in its wider sense—while a third implies quite a loose reference to 'craftsmen' in general.

In most cases, the persons described as 'wise' or as possessing the quality of 'wisdom' are males. Our task will be to examine these words when they are applied to females; and to investigate, through a comparison with their 'male' usages, whether women could or did belong to either of the categories mentioned. We shall examine the stories of two women who were involved in matters of state, to find out whether the activities attributed to these individuals were unique to them or else are indicative of a certain social institution of female counsellors (sections b, c). Then we shall discuss two classes of skilled women—Mourners and Craftswomen (sections d, e). We shall consider the case of Abigail, who is neither considered 'wise', nor is the Hebrew adjective *ḥᵃkāmâ* (feminine) used in her description (section f). Finally we shall examine the curious personification of the abstract concept Wisdom as a woman (section g)—curious because, according to the Old Testament and later Jewish and Christian traditions, as a rule women did not belong to the class of teachers/educators which features so largely in Wisdom literature.

b. *The woman of Tekoa (2 Samuel 14)*

Joab goes to Tekoa and commissions a 'wise woman' from that town, in order to effect a reconciliation between David and Absalom. He knows that David's longing for his son has already overcome his anger (2 Samuel 13.39). Joab himself cannot plead directly on Absalom's behalf, so he approaches the problem indirectly. As it happens, his plan is quite effective (14.20-24).

Who is the 'wise woman' whom Joab chooses for the delicate mission? The text does not supply us with her name. The grammatical form *'iššâ ḥᵃkāmâ*, without the article, can be interpreted in more than one way. It may mean 'any woman who is known to be wise', chosen at random; or 'a certain wise woman' whose reputation—if not her name—is well known. It would seem that the second possibility is the more plausible, for Joab is presented as a calculating man who plots his moves carefully. He is looking for somebody whom David will not readily recognize, but who will nevertheless perform the appointed task well; and the woman of Tekoa is highly suitable for this role. It is not only that she can repeat the words Joab has previously put in her mouth, but also that she does so convincingly. Her ability to achieve what she has set out to do becomes apparent the moment she swings from her fabricated personal complaint (a family's wish to avenge the blood of a murdered son by killing his murderer, the remaining son) to David's personal business (his refusal to let Absalom, the son–murderer, return from exile and assume his position as heir to the throne). While recounting her (imaginary) personal story she manages to enlist David's support by juxtaposing two principles of social order—private blood revenge, and the basic prerogative of central government to impose order through the institutional procedures of the law. This is a political matter, designed to arouse David's interested commitment. As such, the whole affair was probably well planned by Joab; but the skill with which the woman commences to introduce David's problem, her talent for pursuing the analogy between her troubles and the king's through recurrent references to her own case, and, finally, the way she deals with the king when he calls her bluff all point to the fact that she is much more than an accomplished actress who repeats, parrot-like, what Joab has ordered her to say. She has the presence of mind to seize upon a situation, judge it for herself, and manipulate it to her own advantage. These precisely are the qualities which made Joab choose her for this particular assignment. If we were to attempt a definition of this woman's wisdom (using our biblical text as it stands, and rejecting any knowledge which is external to it) we should arrive at the following conclusions. This 'wise' woman can be commissioned to manipulate a person to act the way she wants him to. She achieves that by enlisting the person's cooperation instead of arousing his anger or animosity. She can be counted on for sensing undercurrents of emotions and opinions, and for utilizing them. She can adapt easily to changes in the atmosphere, and redirects these changes according to her purpose through improvization. In short, she is adept in both rhetoric and psychology; her services can be commanded or hired (the text does not specify whether Joab did pay her) in order to mediate in, or influence the course of, personal and political disputes.

c. *The woman of Abel-beth-maacah (2 Samuel 20.14-22)*

Sheba's rebellion, the aftermath of Absalom's revolt against his father David, came to an end at the northern town of Abel. This time, too, Joab was involved in the proceedings: he negotiated for Sheba's head with a local 'wise' woman.

There is nothing strange in the fact that Joab surrounded the city without actually engaging its inhabitants in combat. He obviously hoped to gain his objective, to quash the uprising, through a battle of nerves rather than a civic bloodbath. The presence of the woman (who, like her predecessor, is nameless) is far from surprising: women have always participated in pre-battle skirmishes during a siege and have even taken part in the defence of their town when necessary and expedient. (Cf. Abimelech's death; he was hit by a millstone thrown

at him by an anonymous woman standing on the city wall, Judges
9.53.) It is significant, though, not only that the woman asks for Joab
by name, but also that he answers readily and cooperates with her.
Did everybody have such easy access to David's chief general? Or
was there, from the outset, a special reason for Joab's response to a
woman who, presumably, was unknown to him? For the moment, let
us assume that something in her appearance, demeanour, or perhaps
apparel, engaged his attention. At any rate, Joab treats the 'wise'
woman seriously and, indeed, the outcome justifies his attitude.

The woman begins the dialogue by citing a proverb which,
although now corrupt beyond comprehension, is intended to extol
the wisdom of Abel's people (v. 18). Then she goes on to accuse Joab
of wishing to demolish the town (v. 19). Although she has not
introduced herself formally, the famous general immediately apolo-
gizes: he does not want to harm anyone. All he wants is the rebel's
head (vv. 20-21). The woman commits herself to granting Joab's wish
without hesitation (v. 21). The text states laconically that she appeared
in front of 'all the people', probably either the whole congregation or
the elders' council and, using her 'wisdom', convinced them that the
prevention of imminent destruction and bloodshed is more important
than the obligations of hospitality. Sheba was killed and the siege
stopped at once (v. 21). Again Joab shows himself to be not only a
warrior but also a statesman; he prefers a peaceful solution to a
battle. In this case the local 'wise' woman has achieved the solution
single-handedly, to the relief of both parties.

A few details in the story are especially worth noting. The woman
is widely respected: everybody listens attentively to what she has to
say, from Joab to her fellow townspeople. She has authority and
influence. After assessing the situation, she does not hesitate and
gives Joab an immediate answer to his request. She is as good as her
word: she convinces the assembly that it is imperative to comply with
Joab's demands, and ensures that it is carried out. Therefore, it seems
that she is no ordinary woman. She probably enjoys some kind of a
unique status or reputation. Her position is such that she can
approach the assembly (of which, traditionally, only males are
members) and speak to it. This, even in times of a danger as great as
the one described here, is quite extraordinary. We note that, unlike
the woman who killed Abimelech, our heroine chose to act through
the accepted and official institutions of her town; she uses rational
considerations, persuasion and rhetoric rather than spontaneous

action, and she succeeds in achieving what she has set out to do. Like the 'wise' woman of Tekoa, she uses psychological insight; and both are referred to simply as 'a wise woman' rather than by name. Therefore, we might conclude that they are both professionals, not simply bright individuals; that they are recognized as successful and good at their profession; and that they were famous (which would explain Joab's choice of the Tekoa woman). As members of an institution, they may have worn special garments which immediately identified them as practitioners of this specific occupation (which would explain Joab's readiness to talk with the woman from Abel).

d. *The 'skilled women' of Jeremiah 9.16 (17)*

The word $h^a k\bar{a}m\hat{o}t$ is the plural (feminine) of $h^a k\bar{a}m\hat{a}$, which in the two cases reviewed above has been translated 'wise'. Nevertheless, the context of Jeremiah 9.16-21 (17-22), a call for mourning, excludes the possibility of such a translation. Whereas the two 'wise' women mentioned above distinguished themselves by their rhetoric, good sense and insight, the 'wisdom' of the $h^a k\bar{a}m\hat{o}t$ in this passage consists of their 'skill' (thus the NEB) or 'cunning' (Authorized Version) as mourners.

Professional mourning women are mentioned in a few other Old Testament passages too (Ezekiel 32.16 [twice]; 2 Chronicles 35.25). From our passage itself we learn that women could instruct their daughters and friends in this art (v. 19 [20]). It seems that, as with many professions, membership in this one was exclusive and, to a large extent, hereditary. Women who took up mourning as a vocation had to learn the formulae of their trade. These formulae were recited in funerary services and on similar occasions. In fact, the passage contains an ancient formula which describes death as a god who climbs through windows and steals into the houses of the living:

> Death has climbed in through our windows, it has entered our palaces... (v. 20 [21]).

Cassuto[1] was the first to show that the formula reflects a Ugaritic myth. According to this myth the god Baal keeps the windows of his palace tightly shut, for he fears that his brother Mot—god of death and the underworld—will climb through them and kill Baal's wives. Therefore, the formula antedates much of the earliest Hebrew poetry that has come down to us. A professional mourner, then, had to be learned and well versed in the poetic stock peculiar to her occupation. The 'wisdom' of the mourning women consisted of their vocational skill (this is borne out by the poetic structure of v. 16 [17]: 'mourning women', in the first column of the verse, parallels $h^a k \bar{a} m \hat{o} t$ in the second). Hence, the term $h^a k \bar{a} m \hat{o} t$ here should be translated 'skilled women', not 'wise women'.

As noted earlier, the scope of the Hebrew term applied is quite wide: it may denote 'wise, clever' (2 Samuel 14, 20) as well as 'skilful, possessing practical knowledge of a certain sort' (Jeremiah 9).

We conclude, then, that—as we saw earlier—some women are described as 'wise' because it is recognized that they possess a special status and belong to a specific institution—that of 'wise women'. These women are clever, articulate, involved in the political life of the community—in short, they enjoy a status similar to that of an elder, or a 'wise man'. Other women—as here—are depicted as 'wise' simply because they are adept and skilful in their chosen profession or occupation which—more often than not—is a traditionally feminine one.

e. The 'wise-hearted' women of Exodus 35.25

Another traditionally female occupation is denoted by the application of 'wise' to 'women' (and 'men') within the narrative which deals with the construction of the Tabernacle in the desert. The 'wise-hearted' (thus, literally translated from the Hebrew *hakmat lēb* in the Authorized Version) women are actually spinners and weavers of fine, multi-coloured cloth. The men to whom the same description is applied on numerous occasions within the same narrative (Exodus 28.3; 31.6; 35.10, 35; 36.1, 2, 8) are craftsmen—builders, carpenters, and so on. Therefore, these women belong to the second category delineated above: their 'wisdom' is their skill. It has very little connection with the 'wisdom' that is the combined result of intelligence, experience and rhetoric (the first category).

The use of 'wise-hearted' to mean 'skilled' is peculiar to the Tabernacle narrative of the book of Exodus. The same term, when it appears in biblical wisdom literature, namely Proverbs and Job (Proverbs 10.8; 11.29; 16.21; Job 9.4; 37.24), denotes intelligence, cleverness and good sense, not craftsmanship and skill. We have already noted that 'wise' on its own can mean 'skilful' (as in Jeremiah 9; Exodus 36.4; 2 Chronicles 2.6, 11). Both meanings are included within the range of the Hebrew term, and are applied to the description of males and females alike: the 'wise-hearted' women of Exodus 35.25 are skilful craftswomen who practise traditionally feminine crafts. As such they are much respected—as is the Virtuous Woman of Proverbs 31, that prodigy of industrious wifehood and womanhood.

f. *Abigail (1 Samuel 25.2-42)*

The Abigail story is an immoral but amusing tale which describes how David came to marry her. It happened during the time when David was continuously escaping from King Saul, and after he had already grouped an army of fugitives around him. The chief character is David who, in modern terms, is 'running a protection racket' (vv. 6-8, 15, 21)[2] around the Judaean area of Maon (v. 2), thus feeding himself and his disreputable band. The man whom David claims to be protecting is the wealthy stock breeder Nabal (Hebrew 'the churl'), who in fact rejects David's approach quite rudely (vv. 10-11). The woman who manages to avert the imminent disaster threatened by David's wrath (vv. 21-22) is Nabal's wife Abigail, depicted as 'a beautiful and intelligent woman' (v. 3). Nabal conveniently dies of a stroke a few days later (v. 38), and Abigail becomes David's wife. Let us examine how 'she plays her cards well and wins David as a husband'.[3] Incidentally, the union strengthens David's position as future king, for it constitutes a link between David and the important Calebite tribe of Abigail's first husband.

When the intelligent (Hebrew *ṭôbat śēkel* = 'of good understanding' or 'of good sense') Abigail hears about the incident from her servants, she first packs a sizeable tribute for David and his companions and sends it with her men. She herself follows, riding on her ass.

Like another influential woman, the great lady of Shunem who rushes to meet the prophet Elisha when her son dies, so that Elisha will bring him back to life (2 Kings 4.8-37), Abigail can take the initiative without her husband's consent. Her control of household affairs, and the servant's loyalty to her, are such that Nabal does not even know of her activities until she chooses to tell him the next morning (1 Samuel 25.37). This, together with the fact that she can leave the family estate without a proper chaperone, is a measure of her status and relative independence. Later on we read that she comes to David with 'five maids in attendance' after personally accepting his marriage proposal (vv. 41-42), a detail which, once again, points to her secure economic position and personal independence. This is highly irregular, unconventional and atypical for the patriarchal framework within which she lives.

As in the cases of the two 'wise' women associated with Joab, an important component of Abigail's intelligence is her eloquence. The speech she delivers to David—which, together with her tribute, brings about his reconciliation and their eventual marriage—is a beautifully constructed piece of manipulation, carefully designed to further her own ends (if not, ultimately, those of her husband Nabal). She humbles herself and assumes a modest attitude. She gains David's good will by flattering him and admitting his position as God's favourite (v. 28). She belittles her husband (v. 25), congratulates David on his patience, and asks him to refrain from immediate revenge (v. 26). Like the woman of Tekoa (1 Samuel 14), Abigail talks to David about the blood guilt which might hinder his prosperity later if he chooses to take action against the irresponsible, worthless Nabal now (vv. 29 onwards). She hints that as the real responsibility for the household is hers—which is borne out by her authoritative behaviour—her actions should suffice to cancel out her husband's foolishness. She wishes David long life and success, admits his just claim to the throne of Israel (while King Saul is still the formally anointed ruler), and begs to be remembered when the time comes (vv. 29-31).

David, of course, has no choice but to capitulate. The combination of beauty, eloquence and flattery is too beguiling to be ineffective. He agrees to leave Nabal alone, compliments Abigail on her swift actions (vv. 32-35) and later, after Nabal's death, weds her. So, Abigail's policy successfully solves the short-term problem. At the same time it proves to be a wise long-term policy, for it takes care of Abigail's future, although this is done at the expense of her husband Nabal and Saul, who is the reigning king. Her motive is totally selfish: she saves her household, and we get the distinct impression that she is more interested in the household than in Nabal's personal welfare. There is nothing wrong with that from the point of view of the storyteller, who is on David's side and does not attempt to be impartial. Abigail's cleverness is defined as 'good sense' of the practical variety, a cunning utilized to obtain personal gratification for personal objectives. Although she shares the qualities of intelligence and insight with the 'wise' women associated with Joab (see sections b and c above), she is not a 'wise' woman herself because her scope is limited to her own affairs and does not extend to public affairs. Perhaps the differentiation is hinted at in the choice of (Hebrew) adjective which describes her: Abigail is a woman of 'good sense' (*ṭôbat śēkel*), but not 'wise' (*ḥᵃkāmâ*).

g. *Wisdom personified as a woman (Proverbs 1–9)*

Biblical 'Wisdom literature' (mainly Proverbs, Job, Ecclesiastes, and a number of psalms) belongs to a literary genre, prevalent in the ancient Near East, which is designed to teach and educate towards a successful and profitable way of life.[4]

The genre is directed first and foremost at the young and inexperienced, and supplies instructions of traditional knowledge and practical value. The 'wisdom' transferred from parent to (male) child, from teacher to pupil, prepares the younger person for a successful conventional life within his (mostly upper class) circle. It shows him how to secure a social and economic niche for himself. This 'wisdom' is, by nature, relatively secular. However, in the case of Hebrew tradition a second layer, one which equates wisdom with 'fear of God' (Proverbs 1.7), was later imposed onto the basic concept, thus bringing the wisdom literature of the Old Testament closer to the main stream of Jewish orthodox thought.[5]

One of the peculiarities found in the first collection of Proverbs (chs. 1–9) is the hyperbolic representation of Wisdom and, to a lesser extent, Folly. The two concepts are described in the form of two women, each with her own characteristic attributes. Wisdom (Hebrew *ḥokmâ* or, in two cases, the plural form *ḥokmôt*) is an eloquent women who advertises her wares in the streets and market places (1.20-21). She is a teacher whose job is to instruct the inexperienced and foolish in the right path, the path of life (1.24 onwards). At times she is portrayed as a bride and wife (3.13-18; 4.6-9)[6] whose constant love means life, happiness and success for her man: she is even called 'sister'/'bride' (7.4), like the beloved in the Song of Songs (Song 4.9, 10, 12; 5.1, 2).

Proverbs 8 deals exclusively with Lady Wisdom. She is described in two ways: as a teacher who announces her philosophy of life publicly (vv. 1-21, and similar to ch. 1); and as a divine entity, either God's daughter or a divine attribute (vv. 22-31) which has existed since, or before, the creation of the world and has had a cosmological and governmental function ever since. Clearly, the second of these two personifications belongs to the later stage of wisdom literature, a stage which defines wisdom as a divine rather than a secular concept (as in Job 28.12-28; and see above).

Lady Wisdom of Proverbs 9 shares some characteristics with her personifications considered earlier, albeit with certain substantial additions. She is busy organizing a house-warming dinner party in her new, seven-pillared home. The number seven is known to have had some cultic as well as literary significance. This detail, as well as the festive meal Wisdom offers to her guests, raises the possibility that a cultic act is implied—and so think some of the commentators on the passage. Others find here (9.1-2) a reminiscence of foreign institutions.[7] Be that as it may, this time the lady does not do her own advertising. She sends her maids to public meeting places (v. 3) and they, once again, invite the inexperienced who are in need of education (v. 4). The maids are persuasive; the speech Wisdom puts in their mouths combines promises of an immediate pleasure, the meal, with those of long life and prosperity.

The woman Folly (vv. 13-18) employs a similar technique. She sits in her doorway and tempts passers-by with her rhetorical skill (vv. 14-17). Her promise of pleasure is a trap: because her teachings are immoral, her followers' fate is death (vv. 17-18). However, the means she chooses to seduce her clients is verbal, exactly like her counterpart Wisdom. It must be said, though, that in terms of the literary hyperbole Folly is presented as a less rich, powerful or eloquent figure than her opposite number.

The description of the abstract concept Wisdom (or rather, as we have noted, there are actually two concepts—an original one of secular wisdom, and a secondary one with the Yahwistic concept of 'fear of God' superimposed upon it) in the form of a woman, and in terms of an extended metaphor, is peculiar to the first collection of Proverbs (chs. 1–9). Nowhere else in the Old Testament do we find its like. The grammatical gender of the Hebrew word *ḥokmâ*, 'wisdom', is the feminine. This, perhaps, may have supplied the initial motivation for creating the figure—but it does not explain its development. Some scholars tend to see in Lady Wisdom a reproduction or adaptation of a goddess figure, borrowed from foreign cultures.[8] This opinion fails to clarify why the personified Wisdom figure is unique to Proverbs 1–9. Further, the personification, even if it is a literary device only, an effective and picturesque method of instruction,[9] is not used anywhere else in the Old Testament. The prophet Ezekiel describes the kingdoms of Judah and Israel as two wayward sisters (Ezekiel 23). Zion/Jerusalem is called 'The (virgin) daughter of Zion' by Isaiah, Jeremiah and other prophets, as well as in the Psalms and Lamentations. In the same sources the epithet 'daughter' is extended to refer to other cities and nations—such as Babylon (Isaiah 47.5; 50.42; Psalm 137.8); Egypt (Jeremiah 46.11); and Edom (Lamentations 4.21-22), to name but a few. From Hosea onwards the relationship of *ḥesed* ('love') between God and his chosen people—or the disruption of this relationship—is sometimes described as a marriage bond between a constant man and his often disloyal wife. These various literary conventions, in which a female figure stands for an abstract or collective entity, are too numerous not to be taken into account. Not all of them can be considered the result of a literary loan from cultures outside the Israelite tradition. On the contrary: although unique to Proverbs 1–9, the personification of Wisdom belongs to a convention which is well known and widely used in Old Testament literature. So the question remains: Why does the hyperbole of Lady Wisdom appear in the Proverbs collection only, and what is its specific literary origin?

Within Proverbs 1–9 there are four passages which warn the inexperienced against a 'Foreign Woman'.[10] This Foreign Woman (2.16-19; 5.3-14, 20; 6.24-25; 7.5-27) is a dangerous and immoral seductress, a married but faithless woman, perhaps even a cult prostitute (7.10, 14-17). Her strength lies not so much in her external appearance but—in all the passages—in her eloquence: she is persuasive, her tone is beguiling. This type of woman offers intellectual as well as sexual pleasures. The fact that warnings against her are repeated again and again suggests that the type was extremely attractive to young, naive men of the upper classes, for whose benefit the wisdom instruction is delivered. The woman's charm is especially dangerous since she is unconventional and quick to take the initiative. She goes to the street, picks her unsuspecting victim, charms him with promises of food and sex. Her tongue gets the better of her chosen prey (ch. 7). However, although she promises a good life she actually ensnares her victims in a death-trap (2.18; 5.4ff.; 7.25-27).

Warnings against a Foreign Woman, a stranger who does not see herself as bound by the social conventions of the place she resides in, are also found in extra-biblical sources. We read in an Egyptian Instruction (tentatively dated to the 11th–8th century BC): 'Be on thy guard against a woman from abroad . . . '[11] As we know, Egyptian influence on Proverbs is apparent in subject matter and structure alike. Both sources employ an anxious, urgent tone when they speak about the Foreign Woman.

It must be remembered that the foreign temptress, unlike Wisdom, is not a personification of an abstract concept but a prototype which depicts a kind of woman. It is paradoxical, then, that the wicked female death-trap shares some important features with personified Wisdom, the fountain of life. Both operate from their own home, recruit their clients in public places, use the promise of a (cultic) meal as an attraction, and assure their followers of pleasure and good life. The chief trait they share, over and above the features listed, is their honeyed speech and rhetorical powers.

The differences between Wisdom and the Foreign Woman are obvious. The one is moral, even divine; the other is immoral, corrupt and corrupting. The one is faithful, the other a faithless liar. The one is life, the other—death. Nevertheless, the similarities far outweigh the differences. It seems possible that the prototyped description of the Foreign Woman serves as a literary model for the personified figure of Wisdom, notwithstanding their being antithetical in so many ways. Thus a well-known but negative type is utilized to create a new, original and positive type: Wisdom is, in a sense, the Foreign Woman's daughter. Such is also Woman Folly: her description is even more closely modelled on that of the Foreign Woman, for both are morally negative figures.[12]

h. *Summary*

The two 'wise' women linked with Joab are notable for their good sense, rhetorical prowess, psychological insight, and involvement in the life of the community. They seem to represent either a profession or else a social institution which was forgotten later on.

The 'wise' women of Jeremiah 9 are skilled, professional mourners, and the 'wise-hearted' females of Exodus 35 are craftswomen who practise traditional feminine skills. Hence, there are two categories of 'wise' women:

1. Professionals, whose services can be used to advance the welfare of the community.
2. Women who are skilled in various (traditional) vocations.

Abigail is of 'good sense', but uses her talents to further her own ends only. Therefore, she is not included in either category of 'wise' women.

The personified figure of Lady Wisdom (and, in its wake, that of Lady Folly, Proverbs 1–9), noted for her teaching abilities and rhetorical excellence, is modelled upon the descriptions—within the same literary layer—of the attractive but deadly Foreign Woman. With the latter, as well as with the professional 'wise' woman of Abel and Tekoa, Wisdom shares especially one trait: persuasive eloquence.

Chapter 4

WOMEN POETS AND AUTHORS

a. *General Considerations*

Males and females alike are endowed with the ability to 'tell stories' in poetry and prose, to recite and to transmit them orally or in writing. However, in biblical lore, as well as in other cultures, much more is known about male authors and storytellers than female authors. This seems strange. Stories designed to entertain and instruct have always been invented by women for the benefit of their children. If women do so within the domestic sphere, why not in public? And if they did perform or compose in public, why is this fact unrecorded?

Nevertheless, according to the evidence of the Old Testament very few women did achieve public acclaim for their literary talents throughout the biblical era. Presumably, this is why only a few literary pieces composed by women were apparently preserved in it. One assumes that women, who are not inherently inferior to men from the aspect of literary potential, were so family-bound that their literary efforts (be they educationally or socio-politically motivated) were either publicly unknown, or unrecorded by their male colleagues.

In this chapter we shall examine the scanty information furnished by the Old Testament concerning female authorship and performance of literary compositions. First we shall consider the evidence for female authorship of the Song of Songs or parts thereof, and then proceed to discuss the possible poetic activities of Miriam (Exodus 15) and Deborah (Judges 5).

b. *Female authorship in the Song of Songs*

The Song of Songs is not a 'story'. Neither, as its name implies, is it written in prose. Nevertheless, it is worth including in our discussion of stories about women in Old Testament narrative for three reasons:

it affords possible evidence regarding women authors; it contains narrative sequences of real or archetypal experience; and its chief figure (or figures) is that of a woman (or women).

Many scholars agree that the 'Sublime Song' is a collection of love lyrics and wedding poems, compiled and put together in such a manner that no visible principle of order—apart from its main theme, Love—is discernible. As such it contains materials of diverse chronological and local origins, of different lengths and literary forms.[1] Some poems reflect country life and ideals; others—those of city commerce and the cultural life of Jerusalem. Some allude to the background and geographical factors of the North, yet others to the agricultural realia of the South. Thus, any attempt to determine the circumstantial context of individual poems within the collection is no easy task. There are other problems of interpretation as well. Is the allegorical-sacred interpretation intrinsic to the primary intention of the complete work, or was it later attributed to the profane lyrics in order to make them religiously acceptable? Should the recurrent references to King Solomon, or some of them, be taken seriously[2] or discarded altogether? What were the principles that guided the work of the author(s) and editor(s)? To what extent did she/he/they interfere with the source materials? How many *dramatis personae* can we identify, for it seems that more than one loving couple is involved? These questions, and others, continue to inspire scholarly debate concerning the Song of Songs.[3] Here we shall deal with one question only: Is it possible or plausible that some of the love lyrics—especially those which offer a woman's viewpoint—were actually composed by women?

All in all, the eight chapters of the Song contain 117 verses. Out of these, sixty-one and a half are delivered by a woman speaker; forty by a man speaker; six and a half by choruses of either sex (the 'daughters of Jerusalem', and the rustic woman's brothers); and the remaining nine verses either serve as headings (1.1), or else are impossible to assign with certainty to a male's or female's viewpoint. The distribution of male voices and female voices is presented in the following table:

Distribution of female and male voices in the Song of Songs

Chapter	woman verses	total	man verses	total	choruses verses	total	others verses	total
1	2-7, 12-14, 16-17	11	8-11, 15	5	–	–	1	1
2	1,3-9, 10-13, 16-17	14	2,14	2	–	–	15	1
3	1-5	5	–	–	6?	1	7-11	5
4	16	1	1-5 7-15	14	–	–	6?	1
5	2-8, 10-16	14	1	1	9	1	–	–
6	2-3	2	4-10, 12?	8	1	1	11	1
7	11-14	4	1-10	10	–	–	–	–
8	1-4,5b-7,10,11-12,14	10.5	–	–	5a?8-9,13	3.5	–	–
Total		61.5 verses		40 verses		6.5 verses		9 verses

NOTES:

a. 2,10-13 are spoken from the man's viewpoint, but form a quote within the woman's words.

b. 3,7-11 describes King Solomon's bed, his heroes and wedding. It is difficult to ascribe this poem to either male or female. Perhaps is properly belongs to one of the choruses.

c. 5,2-4 is a dialogue between man and woman, but within the woman's words. 5,9 is uttered by the 'daughters of Jerusalem'.

d. 6,12 - cf. 7,2; 6,1 - cf. 5,9.

e. 8,5a - cf. 3,6: 8,8-9 - attributed to the girl's brothers.

If we want to express the female–male relationship statistically, the female voice(s) account(s) for approximately 53% of the text, while the male voice(s) account(s) for only 34%. The remaining 13% belong to the choruses (6%), or are headings and dubious cases (7%).

This ratio, indeed, is quite surprising. Whatever the provenance of the individual poems or collections—whose boundaries, in many instances, are far from well defined—one would expect them to be mostly male-oriented, for they express emotions nurtured in a decidedly patriarchal society. In literary terms, male dominance may lead us to expect, among other things, that the chief actor(s) and speaker(s) would be men. An author/compiler who chose to include such a high percentage of 'female' love lyrics in the work must have been motivated by the literary merit of the individual poems, not by the socio-ideological coinage prevalent within his society. This, of course, does not necessarily imply that this same author had a feminist bias.[4] Rather, it might indicate that considerations of ultimate authorship, or of the balance between the roles assigned to each sex, did not influence the author/compiler's choice. Conversely, this editor/compiler might be identified as a woman. Such an identification (although hypothetical) would explain why a relatively large portion of the Song deals with feminine emotions while the male is relegated to a secondary position. Unfortunately this last assumption, which can be based on quantitative considerations, has no further evidence to support it.

One should return, then, to the individual poems—even though their boundaries are often blurred—and concentrate one's attention on their contents. Can it be that some or certain poems are not only presented as spoken by a woman or women, but also reflect a woman's emotions and world in such an authentic manner that no man is likely to have written them? If we can show that this is the case, the assumption that at least some portions of the book are authentic female compositions becomes much more plausible.

There are two dream sequences in the Song of Songs, 3.1-4 and 5.2-7. Both are female dreams which describe the quest for the beloved. In the first dream the lady would like to bring her loved one, once found, to her mother's house (as in 8.1-5; see also in 3.11, where Solomon's mother, not his father, is associated with his wedding). The extreme value patriarchal society places on virginity and sexual modesty is present in both dreams, but is especially emphasized in the second one. There the lovesick woman is stripped by the guards for daring to look for her beloved (5.7). The conflicts, contents and symbols of the dream sequences are 'typically female'[5] in terms of modern psychology. Furthermore, had we not known better we would have expected such passages as 3.4 and 8.1—in which the woman wishes to 'adopt' her lover for a brother, so as to make their liaison acceptable and more effective—to reflect a matriarchal social order. On the other hand, the 'brothers' (1.6c; 8.8-9) or guards (3.3; 5.7) act as the woman's keepers. This conforms with her situation—a protected virgin in a male dominated society—but, atypically, she has the last word (8.10).

In general, the love lyrics expressed by the woman/women in the Song of Songs are as fervently sexual and outspoken as the men's. However, there is less humour in the female lyrics: see, for instance, the drunken and humorous poem which describes the dancing Shulamite (7.1-8 and further, vv. 9-10a; some of the images recur in 4.3-5, albeit in a different tone). To this rather hilarious male ribaldry one can compare the serious, traditionally statuesque description of the male lover uttered by the woman (5.10-16). To paraphrase Lord Byron's words, a woman's love is her *raison d'être*, a serious matter not to be fooled with; in contradistinction, a man's love is less central to his being because he can find self-expression not only in love but also in other pursuits. It is not that the male does not feel for the woman—he does, but is capable of laughing at her as well as of being profoundly serious. The woman, alas, thinks her love is no joking matter; this humourless state, if we may risk a generalization at this point, constitutes an editorial comment on female love.

To summarize: after having aired the above considerations, we still are in no position to determine with confidence which portions of the Song of Songs express typical female attitudes with such fidelity that they can be regarded as original compositions by women. My personal guess is that passages such as 1.2-6, 3.1-4, 5.1-7, and 5.10-16 are so essentially feminine that a male could hardly imitate their tone and texture successfully. After all, there is no reason to maintain that women were not recognized as great poets in ancient Israel. Deborah and Miriam were (see below); and the 'singers' of both sexes mentioned in Ecclesiastes (2.8) probably composed as well as performed their own poems and those of others.

c. *Miriam (Exodus 15) and Deborah (Judges 4–5)*

Exodus 15 contains a poem which celebrates the passage of the Israelites through the Red Sea. An introductory verse depicts Moses as the leader and the initiator of the male chorus that performs the poem:

> Then Moses and the Israelites sang this song to the Lord . . . (v. 1)

Miriam, in her capacity as the leader of the women's chorus, supervises another performance:

> And Miriam the prophetess, Aaron's sister [!], took her tambourine, and all the women followed her, dancing to the sound of tambourines; and Miriam sang them this refrain . . . (vv. 20-21a)

Although the English translation here quoted (NEB) seems straightforward, it reproduces a Hebrew text that is far from clear. The translation, for better or for worse, irons out some obvious difficulties (like the translation of Hebrew *šîr*, 'song', as 'refrain', v. 21; and see below). A closer look at the Hebrew passage reveals several difficulties. Should we assume that Moses merely acts as chief singer, or is he the author of the poem as well? What is the women's role? Do they join the men during the recital itself, or do they just repeat the refrain and supply the musical accompaniment? Perhaps they repeat the poem after it has first been performed, together with music and jubilant dancing? And consequently does Miriam share a position of literary leadership and/or authorship with Moses, or is she merely his female echo? And why is she called Aaron's, not Moses' sister? Because the Masoretic (Hebrew) text (= MT) is ambiguous, some attention should be paid to these points.[6]

If we assume that the Song of the Sea was composed and first delivered by Moses, then Miriam's recital must be a repeat performance. On the other hand, what is the sense in delivering two separate performances of the same spontaneous (according to the biblical framework) poem? The MT tells us that Miriam's poetic and musical leadership is confined to members of her own sex, and that—chronologically—it succeeds that of Moses. Nevertheless, she cites the beginning of the poem (not a repeated refrain, which is not supported by the Hebrew text; the NEB translation quoted above is unacceptable) as if she intended to recite it fully—although there is no need, within the MT, to repeat it. Indeed, the Hebrew word used in v. 21—from the root *'nh*—may mean 'answer', as well as 'repeat' or simply 'sing'. The NEB probably translates as it does in order to resolve some of the ambiguities mentioned above by depicting Moses as sole author of the poem.

Let us explore an alternative possibility: that Miriam may once have been regarded as the original author/performer. The ambiguity or tension in the MT perhaps resulted from the fusion of two distinct traditions concerning the question of authorship. If this indeed was the case, then the biblical narrator was faced with a dilemma and might have decided to take the easy way out by harmonizing the two traditions, thus making Moses the author and Miriam his female echo. In this way he solved his problem, or thought he did. Indeed, women probably did repeat victory poems sung by returning warriors when they welcomed the heroes. However, we might explore the possibility that women not only repeated but also composed poems of military victory. If we manage to show that they actually did, then Miriam's authorship of the Song of the Sea might seem a more plausible tradition.

The fact that women did compose victory poems with which they greeted returning military heroes or armies is beyond dispute. Two relevant examples are the premature victory poem attributed to the princesses who attended Sisera's mother, which is to be found within the Song of Deborah (Judges 5.29-30, where the Hebrew verb introducing the poem—'nh—is the same as the one used to describe Miriam's poetic and musical activity); and the poem sung by the women to celebrate David's victory over the Philistines (1 Samuel 18.7, also referred to in 1 Samuel 21.12 and 28.5, again with the same Hebrew verb, and to the accompaniment of music and dancing). In both cases it seems quite safe to assume that the female singers are the authors of the poetic sayings as well as their performers, or that they are responsible for the application of well-known formulae to a specific hero—as they probably did in David's case. Deborah is depicted as senior (first-mentioned) co-singer and, therefore, most probably as at least co-author of the victory poem in Judges 5 (see below). Hence there is nothing to prevent us from thinking that as a leader of women, one of whose usual functions is to cheer the troops after a military event, a woman such as Miriam could have composed and performed a poem designed to celebrate the occasion (or adapted an existing poem to the specific event, which calls for some poetic creativity too).

It is worth noting that Miriam, who is here depicted as a leader of females, elsewhere fights for wider recognition as a national leader (Numbers 12). Even here (Exodus 15.20) she is called 'prophetess', although the exact nature of her prophetic abilities is not explained. Numbers 12 tells us how Miriam and Aaron—in that order—utilize a family dispute concerning a Cushite wife Moses took (v. 1) for political ends. They attempt to obtain a greater share of responsibility and authority by citing Moses' conduct on the one hand, and claiming to be Moses' equals in prophetic authenticity on the other hand (v. 2). God intervenes and the attempt fails. That Miriam was the initiator of the offensive action against Moses we learn from the outcome: she is punished, then saved by Moses' plea on her behalf (vv. 9-15), while Aaron remains unscathed. The conflict, by and large, is a power struggle between Miriam and Moses. God is on Moses' side, and therefore she loses. Nevertheless, she felt confident enough to bid for the supreme position of community leadership. In so doing she does not cite her alleged blood kinship with Moses himself, but regards prophetic gifts equal to Moses' as the basis for her challenge (according to Exodus 15 she is a prophetess). The conclusion we might draw is that Miriam was an important enough figure in her own right—not only just a leader of women, not only just a woman identified as Moses' or Aaron's sister—to wish for greater authority (see below, Chapter 5).

Before the monarchy became institutionalized, there existed in ancient Israel a convention of depicting founding fathers and community leaders as persons of many talents and diverse capabilities. Standard features attributed to outstanding personalities are those considered useful or essential for the realization of governmental authority. The list of desirable traits included a 'spirit of prophecy' which assures the leader of divine inspiration and a direct line to God, sound judgment, juridical knowledge and the ability to administer justice, military prowess, cultic responsibilities, the ability to inspire loyalty and respect, and finally, the gifts of oratory, rhetoric, and literary composition (perhaps even proficiency in music). All of these, or most of them, are attributed to several male leaders and to two female leaders. Thus Abraham (Genesis 20.7), Aaron (Exodus 7.1), Moses (Numbers 12; Deuteronomy 34.10), Samuel (1 Samuel 3.20; 9.9), Miriam (Exodus 15.20) and Deborah (Judges 4.4) are all 'prophets', and King Saul prophesies (1 Samuel 11.19, 24). Abraham carries on a legal argument with God (Genesis 18). Moses acts as a supreme and, at first, the only judge; then, with the aid of his father-in-law, he establishes a juridical hierarchy in the desert community (Exodus 18; a different version appears in Deuteronomy 1). Samuel (1 Samuel 7.15-17) and his sons (1 Samuel 1–2), and Deborah (Judges 4.4) are local judges. Abraham (Genesis 14), Jacob (Genesis 48.22), Moses, Joshua, Deborah, Saul, and David are all described—at least at times—as military leaders. As for cultic activities, Abraham and Jacob establish several cultic shrines (e.g. Bethel and Beersheba).

Moses acts as intermediary between God and man and is a frequent and intimate witness to the divine presence, although proper priestly functions are conducted by his brother Aaron. Samuel grows up in the Shiloh temple, and succeeds Eli's descendants as chief priest there (1 Samuel 2 onwards). Saul comes into conflict with Samuel (1 Samuel 13) because he infringes the latter's cultic responsibilities. A strong, if rather late, tradition ascribes the establishment of the Jerusalem cultus to David (1 Chronicles 13–29); otherwise, this is attributed to Solomon. Earlier traditions, however, name David's sons as priests (2 Samuel 8.18); not until the young monarchy is established, from King Solomon onwards, are kingship and priesthood completely separated. The late story about King Uzziah, who was allegedly smitten with 'leprosy' for attempting to officiate in the Temple (2 Chronicles 26.18-21), is indicative of this trend; and let us note that Miriam is similarly punished for her transgression against Moses in Numbers 12. Women, however distinguished and outstanding as leaders, are excluded from officiating in the cult; Miriam and Deborah are no exceptions to this rule.

There are many examples of literary pieces attributed to community leaders. Jacob's last act as the head of the family is to deliver to his sons a poem which deals with their future destiny (Genesis 49). Moses claims that leadership is out of the question for him because he is not a man of words (Exodus 4.10; 6.12, 30), so his brother Aaron is appointed to be his spokesman (4.14, 17; 7.1-2). Nevertheless, Moses is to 'put the words' in Aaron's mouth (4.15). Contrary to Moses' claims here, other traditions attribute to him not only rhetorical, but also literary gifts. Thus the Song of the Sea is attributed to him (Exodus 15.1) together with other literary blocks and passages.[7] Joshua delivers a number of persuasive speeches (Joshua 22–24); although he is no prophet, his communication with God is established. Samuel is a man of oratorical skill (1 Samuel 8.11-18; 12.1-25; and more). King David composes a poem lamenting the death of Saul and Jonathan (2 Samuel 1), has great musical talents (1 Samuel 16.18 and elsewhere), and is traditionally considered the author of many Psalms. King Solomon is traditionally the author of Ecclesiastes, Proverbs, and the Song of Songs. Deborah shares a victory poem together with Barak (Judges 5). Within this poem itself she features as the more dominant figure: for instance, her name is mentioned three times (vv. 7, 12, 15) to Barak's twice (12, 15), and the poem is structured around its two leading women, Deborah and Jael (see Chapter 5 below). Miriam too, we might recall, sings to celebrate an act of deliverance (Exodus 15). Our task is to investigate whether a credible tradition which considered her as the original author of the poem underlies the present Hebrew text of Exodus 15.

In the preceding paragraphs we have gathered the attributes which make up the character profile of the Ideal Leader. It is, perforce, a composite profile in which different traditions are fused into one literary unity. Thus the Ideal Leader's full list of characteristics will include military, priestly, juridical, prophetic, rhetorical, and literary abilities. As we have seen, Moses is the only leader who conforms fully to the ideal. All other leaders, despite their greatness, do not possess all the features listed but only some or most of them, in accordance with their personal merit. Abraham, Jacob, Aaron, Joshua, Samuel, Saul and David all come short of the Mosaic model, although—to a greater or lesser degree—they share some of its features. Oratorical and literary talents, however, are present in most cases.

The two great female figures of pre-monarchical Israel, Deborah and Miriam, fit into the same category of great leaders. The only sphere that is out of bounds for them from the outset is the priesthood. Deborah is a well-loved and respected local judge, planner of military strategy, prophetess, and co-author—if not sole author—of a victory poem. Miriam aspires to political leadership on the national scale; she is well respected (Numbers 12) as prophetess and singer of the Song of the Sea (Exodus 15). It is conceivable that both—Deborah and Miriam—could have been responsible for the authorship, not just the performance, of the poems with which their names are associated. In much the same way, other literary compositions are linked to names of male leaders, from Jacob to King David. It seems that within the present, male-orientated framework of the text, the women leaders are not permitted to have the distinction of original authorship. Deborah recites her poem together with Barak. Miriam echoes Moses' words in her capacity as the women's leader. Both stories stress the opinion that women, even though they attain a high degree of political involvement and achievement, remain women—and Jewish Midrash elaborates this point further. As such, these female leaders are not depicted as independent figures; they are either led by men or have to share the leadership with them, in the literary area as well as in others. In other words, they are not presented as possessing a talent for the independent poetic creativity which is almost a standard feature of their male counterparts.

d. *Conclusions*

Many verses of the Song of Songs are put in a woman's mouth, and/or delivered from a woman's point of view. There is no reason why a male author should not be able to recreate an authentic representation of female emotions through his psychological and poetic insights. However, some passages are so typically feminine that female authorship is a distinct possibility—especially since women singers and chanters are mentioned on various occasions, joyous as well as sad, as performers and composers.

Miriam's and Deborah's names are linked, as co-performers or co-authors together with a male figure, to two great victory poems. Evidence derived from defining the literary model of the Ideal Leader before the time of King Solomon suggests that oratorical and literary skills are an important component of the leader's inventory of abilities. There is no reason to confine these features to male leaders alone. Therefore both women—the greatest female leaders in pre-monarchical Israel—were probably conceived of by some traditions as more independent and autonomous than they were by the mainstream of the Hebrew Bible. This applies to their literary abilities as well as to other activities associated with their public roles (see the next Chapter).

Chapter 5

PROPHETESSES

a. *General considerations*

Apart from 'prophesying' women (see Chapter 6), the Old Testament
acknowledges very few women as legitimate prophetesses. These are
Miriam and Deborah during the pre-monarchical period; Huldah
during the reign of Josiah, in the second part of the seventh century
BC; and Noadiah in Nehemiah's time, the fifth century BC. Anonymous
women who belong to prophetic bands, like those who appear in the
Elijah and Elisha cycle of narratives, are but companions to the
prophets. Nowhere are they described as possessing prophetic powers
themselves; hence, they are excluded from our discussion. The same
applies to Isaiah's 'prophetess' (Isaiah 8.3), presumably his wife,
whose sole 'prophetic' role is to give birth to a child who will be given
a symbolic name. On the other hand, two New Testament women
are included in our list: Anna, an old Temple prophetess who
foresees Jesus' destiny (Luke 2.36); and a false prophetess whose
figure is modelled upon that of Queen Jezebel (1 Kings 16–2 Kings 9),
and who is referred to in Revelation 2.20-23.

By definition, prophetic activities ascribed to women should not be
different from those attributed to their male counterparts. Therefore,
a few remarks concerning the nature of prophecy in general are in
order at this point. A prophetic saying can be delivered to an
individual, or to a group of people. It may assume the form of
oracular speech, or be expressed by means of ecstatic behaviour,
dreams, signs, symbolic action—all of which might disclose glimpses
into the future, or else opaque hints requiring some kind of interpretation. The contents may range from encouragement to warnings of
doom and from socio-political to religio-moral matters. Some prophets,
notably the pre-classical ones such as Moses, Aaron, Elijah, Elisha,
and a few anonymous 'men of God', perform outright miracles. The
common denominator for all these activities is that they are under-

stood to spring from a direct and legitimately claimed divine inspiration. This inspiration is bestowed upon the prophet even against his wishes, and he has no choice but to accept the divine mission. As we shall see, no Old Testament prophetess is ever reported to have performed a miracle. Apart from that, her activity may correspond to any given type of male prophecy.

In the pre-monarchical, as well as in the early monarchical era, mechanical divination and oracle seeking were a priestly prerogative. The priests used such aids as the *ephod* (described in Exodus 28.6 onwards; for a possible case of consulting the *ephod* in order to obtain a yes-no oracle, see 1 Samuel 23.1-6) or the *Urim* and *Thummim* (Exodus 28.30), whose identification remains obscure. Nothing much can be gathered about these activities apart from the general notion that the Urim and Thummim were probably 'lots with which an oracle could be produced in answer to a question put in the form of two alternatives', and which was 'an old piece of priestly activity'[1]. The principle is similar to divination in other Near Eastern cultures: God's word is actively sought for by means of a mechanical act, or the interpretation of a natural phenomenon. It is important to note that this (priestly) mode of seeking God's counsel later fell into insignificance and even oblivion—hence the sketchy and vague information concerning the practice—while the importance of prophets who delivered the divine Word increased. Thus the priests lost their monopoly as mediators between God and men.

Since Israelite women were never allowed to officiate in the cult, they were excluded from this priestly role of oracle-seeking. In other Mediterranean lands, from ancient Mesopotamia to Egypt and Greece, mechanical divination was practised by male and female cult officials alike. In later Israel it almost disappeared; divination practised by laymen and laywomen always tended to be frowned upon and judged to be sorcery. Women are accused of being enthusiastic practitioners of sorcery and strongly condemned because of it—but this already brings us within the scope of the next chapter.

Finally, a phenomenon similar to Israel's prophecy of the Word apparently existed at Mari. Professionals of at least two classes and spontaneous 'prophets' of both sexes delivered oracles and dream accounts concerning matters of state to kings and high officials.[2] For our part, it is important to note that women took part in this 'prophetic' activity, and that their sex did not discredit their inspiration or message. This, indeed, is the situation in the Old Testament too: prophetesses are few but their reputation, once established, is beyond dispute. The question is, what types of prophetic activities were practised by these outstanding biblical prophetesses?

b. *Huldah (2 Kings 22.14-20 = 2 Chronicles 34.22-28)*

When King Josiah's priests found 'the Book' in the Temple, which probably contained the nucleus of the Book of Deuteronomy, the king sent emissaries to seek God's guidance. The situation, he feared, was hopeless: the people had never behaved in accordance with the divine Word, and now divine retribution—realistically conveyed in a series of curses, similar to or identical with Deuteronomy 28.15 onwards—would inevitably befall them. The officials went to a woman prophet, Huldah.

Most biblical commentators have pointed out that this choice of a prophet is odd. Why not seek God's counsel from Jeremiah or Zephaniah, both prophetically active at the time, rather than an otherwise unknown woman? Perhaps the officials expected that an interview with her would be less embarrassing than one with either of her canonical counterparts;[3] or else Huldah, whose teachings have not been preserved, may have been more respected than her colleagues were during her lifetime. 'We have to remind ourselves that judgments upon personalities and their part in history vary between that of contemporaries and that of posterity.'[4] According to Jewish tradition the two southern gates to the Temple Mount were called the Huldah Gates (Mishnah, Middoth 1.3). If this tradition be sound, then it lends more credibility to Huldah's stature not only during her own lifetime, but also in succeeding generations down to the Second Temple Era. Jewish Midrash too found the choice of Huldah odd, and offered alternative explanations for it: Jeremiah was busy at the time; and Huldah herself, although a woman, was related through her husband to Joshua, so her pedigree was illustrious enough for the job.[5] The biblical text itself goes to great lengths in describing the genealogy and temple function of Huldah's husband, as if these details serve not only to identify the prophetess but also to lend her words authority and credibility. There are minor differences between the Kings and the Chronicles accounts on this point (see commentaries), but they are immaterial; and the pedigree remarks themselves have no significance beyond the realm of easy identification. Huldah's authority rests with the contents of her divinely inspired message:

ultimately its impact is related neither to her husband's position nor to her sex. However, it is interesting to note that Huldah's name is associated with the Temple, although only through her marriage, like those of other great prophets (Isaiah and Ezekiel, for example).

In the best tradition of Isaiah, Jeremiah, Amos, and Hosea, Huldah is fully committed to her unpopular role. She is involved in matters of state, for she delivers an oracle to the king's emissaries, and she does that fearlessly and directly. Her words foresee the destruction of Jerusalem, although Josiah himself will die in peace (2 Kings 22.20; 2 Chronicles 34.38). The last prophetic detail did not come to pass: Josiah died in the Battle of Megiddo (2 Kings 23.29-30; 2 Chronicles 35.20-24) in 609 BC. The non-fulfilment of Huldah's final prophecy marks it as a genuine political prediction delivered prior to the events it refers to. The king, for his part, does accept the oracle as an authoritative message. Thus Huldah plays quite an important role in the institution of Josiah's reform although, like all women, she is actually excluded from officiating in the cult itself.

c. *Noadiah (Nehemiah 6.14)*

Nehemiah's attempt to build up the wall of Jerusalem (in the second half of the fifth century BC), although successful, was opposed and hindered by factions and by individuals. His memoirs, naturally, present his own point of view and condemn his opponents'. We do not know whether his account is accurate, or perhaps exaggerated so as to enhance the impact of his achievement.[6] Among other adversaries, Nehemiah refers to 'prophets' (Nehemiah 6.7-14) who act against him.

Nehemiah accuses his enemies of saying that he has hired prophets to proclaim himself king over Judah (v. 7), which he did not do. The prophet Shemaiah tried to convince him to hide within the Temple, but Nehemiah recognized that Shemaiah's oracle was not a genuine divine word and refused. Furthermore, Nehemiah suspected that the prophet had been hired to trip him up (vv. 10-13). Finally, he concludes his complaint by invoking God's wrath on the heads of his political foes and on the prophets, who were apparently headed by the prophetess Noadiah.

The information we obtain from the text is, as we see, scanty and one-sided. We learn that the prophets are associated with the Temple (again); that their services can be hired for political ends; that they are involved in political activities; that they take sides in a political dispute; and that Nehemiah suspects them of being 'false prophets', in the sense that the oracles they deliver are not divinely inspired.

Noadiah is the only one of the prophets, apart from Shemaiah, who is mentioned by name. This is probably a measure of her importance and political power. Nothing more is known about her deeds, character, or personal history. Is the reference to her, and to Huldah, sufficient to conclude that 'it seems probable that the orders of prophets regularly included some women'?[7] It seems to me that this generalization is unwarranted by the evidence of the text.

d. *Miriam (Exodus 15, Numbers 12)*

The first tradition to mention Miriam by name (Exodus 15.20) grants to her the status of prophetess. Another tradition (Numbers 12) tells how she and Aaron (in this order; Numbers 12.1) claim a degree of prophetic competence similar to Moses'. Miriam fails in this attempt, is punished for her aspirations, and saved by Moses' intervention on her behalf. In spite of the grave rebuke, which reaffirms Moses' status as the greatest prophet among his contemporaries and future generations, it is not explicitly stated that Miriam—and Aaron—are not prophets at all. Nevertheless, no hint as to the nature of Miriam's prophetic activity has been preserved in biblical sources. In contrast, more is known about Aaron's prophecy; for instance, he aids Moses in performing miraculous acts (Exodus 7.19 onwards). How, then, is the application of the attribute 'prophetess' to Miriam to be explained?

We have already pointed out (Chapter 4, section c) that prophetic powers of various sorts are attributed to a number of premonarchical leaders, and that this attribute is a regular feature in the Ideal Leader model. Hence, a partial answer to our puzzle might stem from this almost stereotyped description of public figures as prophets, although in Miriam's case there is no further evidence of prophetic activity. Another possible explanation, put forward by M. Noth, refers to the wider problem of the Miriam–Aaron traditions, and is equally applicable to our specific discussion. 'Aaron and Miriam belong in the tradition to the group of those figures surrounding Moses about whom only remnants of an originally much richer tradition remains, and whose originally independent role we can no longer detect. In time they were made relations of Moses.'[8] Noth further assumes that Miriam 'should thus presumably be characterized as an ecstatic' because 'ecstasy and [cultic] song belonged closely together in ancient Israel . . . '[9] This last statement may be correct but, if applied to Miriam, should be applied to Moses himself, and to all other leaders who are said to have possessed poetic and musical as well as prophetic gifts.

e. *Deborah (Judges 4–5)*

Like Huldah, Deborah is identified as 'wife of', in this case, Lappidoth (4.4), about whom no further information is supplied. Even more than Miriam, Deborah conforms to the stereotype of the multi-talented Great Leader. She is a local judge, and has long been considered the possible authoress of the victory poem assigned to her (ch. 5), which follows the prose narrative describing the battle (ch. 4). (In Exodus we find a similar arrangement: the poem—ch. 15—which follows and celebrates the victory of the prose story—ch. 14—differs from the latter in some points, and is associated with a woman.) Deborah is so well respected that Barak would not undertake the military assignment unless she accompanied him (4.8). Her acceptance assured him that her popularity—much greater than his own—would serve to sanction the military endeavour. In that sense, Deborah shared military responsibility: if we wish to translate the situation into modern terms Deborah is the politician responsible for military affairs, and Barak is her general or chief of staff. Furthermore, the oracle she delivers to Barak, who is summoned to her and obeys her command to come (v. 6), contains the outline of the military campaign (vv. 6-7). In ch. 5 her role is even more pronounced, and Barak's is weaker. Therefore Deborah's derogatory remark, to the effect that because Barak wants her to join him a woman (Jael) will determine the ultimate outcome of the battle (4.9), seems out of character.

Of the two partners, Deborah is the initiator, the brains, the inspiration, Barak the second-in-command, the executive arm. This state of affairs is even more apparent in the poem (ch. 5) than in the prose narrative (ch. 4). A plausible explanation for the discrepancy in describing Deborah's role might stem from the fact that the poem is older and, by virtue of being a poem, much more rigid and relatively less changeable. On the other hand the prose narrative is later and much more fluid by nature, and hence could be modified to present opinions and versions concerning Deborah that were less favourable to her, but glorified Barak's part. The poem, however, is more difficult to tamper with. Its finely structured plan posits Deborah and Jael as the two faces of feminine victory, the political-intellectual together with the sexual aspect; and the two of them are juxtaposed with Sisera's mother and her princesses (5.28-30). The poem gives very little information about how Barak and his warriors defeated the Canaanites: some lines are devoted to various tribes and their behaviour during the emergency (vv. 13-18); others describe the battle as a miracle, not the result of skill and good planning (vv. 19-23). The bulk of the poem, however, is devoted to its female heroines (vv. 7a, 12b, 24-30)—in the sense that they are its focal point. Therefore, any attempt to change or diminish Deborah's (and Jael's) role in the poem would have upset the fine balance of the poetic structure. This consideration, coupled with the force of tradition, was probably responsible for the preservation of Judges 5 as a female-orientated text. We shall return to this subject later, within the discussion of literary female stereotypes (Part II, Chapter 11). For the time being, let us return to Deborah's prophetic activity (Judges 4.4, 6-7).

Unlike Miriam, Deborah's prophetic powers are borne out by the fact that, according to her own claim, she receives a divine oracle which she passes on *verbatim* to the indicated recipient, Barak. We are not told how she has received the oracle, whether by dream, by entering an ecstatic state or by any other means. No introductory formula, such as ' . . . and the word of Yahweh came to . . . ' actually appears in the text. Rather, Deborah claims divine guidance when she gives Barak the plan of his mission. Her claim is accepted as valid, so much so that Barak considers her presence in his camp as an essential guarantee of success. Presumably, in this way he ensures that both divine will and popular support are on his side.

The nature of Deborah's military message is interesting, for it contains much more than a yes/no counsel sought sometimes before embarking on a campaign or battle. In Keilah, David gets direct instructions from God through yes/no answers by consulting the priestly *ephod* (1 Samuel 23). Ahab and Jehoshaphat do not get more explicit instructions when the ecstatic false prophets encourage them to attack Ramoth Gilead (1 Kings 22). Deborah's oracle, however, is a set of directives that—if followed—are supposed to ensure a successful campaign. Thus, her prophecy is similar to the one pronounced by an anonymous prophet to Ahab on the occasion of the king's battle against Ben-hadad, king of Aram (1 Kings 20.13-15). No divine intervention beyond the preliminary stage of instruction is necessary. The plan is so devised as to involve a minimum of risk for the Israelite participants, with no scope for miraculous deliverance. In both of the analogous cases the prophet or prophetess assures the future victor of the successful outcome before the event. Another feature common to the two accounts (Judges 4 and 1 Kings 20) is that none of the designated leaders (Barak and Ahab) has sought God's counsel on the specific occasion. A recurrent literary pattern emerges. A prophet (Deborah, the anonymous prophet) approaches a warrior (Barak, Ahab) without being asked, and acts as God's messenger. The message contains a strategic plan and the promise of success. The military leader adopts the plan, organizes his troops accordingly, and destroys the enemy. The man/woman of God does not actively participate in the military action beyond the planning stage—even Deborah, who accompanies Barak, does not take part in the operation itself. The prophecy is fulfilled, and nothing more is known about the messenger's prophetic activities.

Therefore, it is not surprising that no other instance of Deborah's prophetic powers is to be found in biblical literature. Later generations, though, sought to supplement this lack; the ancient Sages had many things to say about the prophetess. But as the text stands, we have to conclude that Deborah's role as prophetess—as well as author—is closely linked with her charismatic reputation and leadership on this particular occasion. We have just this one *ad hoc* example of her prophetic activity (ch. 4). Finally, let us note that no mention of prophetic activity on her part is made in the poem (ch. 5): there she is depicted (depicts herself?) as a leader, but not as a prophetess.

f. *New Testament prophetesses: Anna, and the 'false prophetess'*

Anna the prophetess (Luke 2.36-38) is described in some detail. The saintly woman is an Israelite from the North (v. 36), an old widow (v. 37). She never leaves the Jerusalem Temple and leads a life of self-denial, fasting, and praying (v. 37). When the baby Jesus is first brought to the Temple by his parents she delivers a prophecy about his destiny.

Anna is presented as an ascetic. Her extreme religiosity sets her far apart from Old Testament prophets and prophetesses; even Jeremiah's life and behaviour seem less devout by comparison. However, a few features are common to Anna and her biblical predecessors. Like Deborah—and a number of male prophets—Anna's message is described as spontaneous and unsolicited by the relevant party. Secondly, the message is treated as an amazing piece of information, but genuine and divinely inspired. Thirdly, the woman is a well-known figure, and her reputation enhances the credibility of her prophecy. Finally, no other prophecy is attributed to her (as is the case with Deborah).

The figure of the Jezebel-like, self-styled false prophetess from Thyatira (Revelation 2.20-23) is aptly modelled after the Old Testament description of her namesake (2 Kings 9.22, for instance). She is accused of teaching harlotry and pagan fertility rites (v. 20). Because she refuses to repent (v. 21), she will be made into an example of severe punishment (vv. 22-23). What her 'prophecy' consists of we do not know. The text dismisses her claim without actually referring to any specific activity on her part. Similarly, in Acts 21.8-9 we read that Philip the evangelist of Caesarea had four virgin or 'unmarried' (thus NEB) daughters who had the gift of prophecy or prophesying. Again, what this 'gift' implies is not specified.

g. *Summary*

Huldah acts as a political prophetess whose counsel is sought and heeded by Josiah.

Noadiah is named by Nehemiah as his chief prophetic adversary. It is possible that she belongs to a band which offers its prophetic services for hire.

Miriam fails in her bid for recognition as Moses' equal in political leadership and prophetic status. Otherwise, no information concerning the nature of her prophetic powers or activities is available. Deborah delivers a single military oracle. This oracle contains a set of instructions for winning a battle. It is obeyed and fulfilled. Apparently, this alone is sufficient for establishing or perpetuating a prophetic reputation. The attribution of prophecy to both Miriam and Deborah is in keeping with the 'Great Leader' type to which they belong.

Anna's personality is that of an ascetic. She is a temple prophetess whose one and only preserved oracle concerns Jesus. In personality and description she is totally different from Huldah, Noadiah, Miriam and Deborah. The 'false prophetess' is a practitioner of a fertility cult. The nature of her prophetic activity is not dwelt upon.

The few biblical prophetesses—much fewer than male prophets—prove by their existence that the prophetic vocation was not out of bounds for women: they could become authoritative and respected mouthpieces for divinely inspired messages. However, their number is small. In some cases their status is described as if it were derived from that of their husbands (Huldah, Deborah) or another male relative (Miriam). In others the prophetic skill is an additional item in an inventory of features attributed to a popular female leader (Miriam, Deborah), which means that they are not distinguished chiefly—or only—for being prophetesses. Only single oracles uttered by women have been preserved. Everything points to the conclusion that although prophetesses were accepted and acknowledged as such (in pre-monarchical as well as monarchical, post-exilic, and New Testament times), their significance—when compared to that of their male colleagues—was marginal.

Chapter 6

MAGICIANS, SORCERERS AND WITCHES

a. *General considerations*

Officially, the Old Testament condemns all magic, sorcery and witchcraft. Various practices which go under these headings—and which are denoted by diverse terms—are regarded as foreign, and alien to the Hebrew spirit. And yet, magic and even witchcraft did exist within Israelite religion—not only within the popular folk systems of beliefs and practices but also within the 'higher' stratum of the official cult. This apparent contradiction, the dialectical phenomenon of denial and acceptance which exist side by side within synchronous ideological states, is commonly found in other well-developed religious systems. Historical and geographical factors, together with the ever-present human aspiration to peep into the future and acquire control of the paranatural, largely account for this phenomenon.

Magic was part and parcel of all great Eastern religions,[1] although a distinction was made between benevolent magic, which was approved of, and malevolent magic, which was forbidden and punishable by law. The Old Testament usually rejects magic altogether, thus attempting to preserve the uniqueness of its faith. On the other hand, many features of magic did infiltrate into it through various channels and were put to old and new uses. The evidence of recurrent biblical exhortations against magic and sorcery shows that these practices existed in Hebrew society throughout the Old Testament era, since cultural contiguity with other nations can never be absolutely avoided. At times of greater cultural mingling or proximity—as during the conquest of Canaan, or the time of the Babylonian Exile—the danger of assimilation and acceptance of magical principles grew, and with it the vehement rejection and the volume of the warnings against them.

When magic, witchcraft and sorcery are associated with foreign pagan cults—which is often the case—they are described by the usual derogative terms employed to discredit these cults. A good example is Jehu's description of Jezebel (2 Kings 9.22) as a witch and a whore, where the latter epithet alludes to the queen's role as patroness of the Baal fertility cult. Other passages, early and late alike, are less loaded with emotion. They depict foreigners such as Balaam (Numbers 23–24), the Philistine priests (1 Samuel 6), and Egyptian and Mesopotamian courtiers (Genesis 47; Exodus 7–9; Daniel 1.20; 2.20) as magicians whose power in performing miracles, foreseeing the future, or changing the course of future events is not to be doubted. Some of these passages (Exodus, Numbers, Daniel) teach us that the God of Israel has greater powers than the foreign gods in whose name these magicians operate. Hence Moses and Aaron defeat the Egyptians through tricks similar to theirs but more spectacular; Balaam is compelled to do God's will; Daniel and his friends are involved in a series of saving miracles. It is stressed that the magical properties bestowed on Moses, Aaron, Balaam and Daniel stem from divine inspiration; and that they are given to them for a specific purpose, usually as a tool of polemics against foreigners. Magic is not, so we are told, a 'natural' or indigenous trait of Hebrew religion. Rather, it is an esoteric trait, to be utilized and displayed when the need arises. Then God, who fully controls magic as he does everything else, lets it be used. Otherwise, no Hebrew man or woman should practise magic through his/her own initiative, since its effectiveness (even when it stems from pagan beliefs) cannot be denied and might be put to irresponsible uses.

What is actually meant by 'magic', 'witchcraft', 'sorcery', and the many Old Testament terms which correspond, fully or partially, to the English ones? The borderlines between the terms are rather fluid, and a certain amount of overlap in denotation is unavoidable. As a result, it is difficult to assign a particular technical meaning to each term. The best guide for understanding any specific 'magical' activity is to follow the particular context it appears in rather than to assign a general meaning to it, and even this method is sometimes fruitless. Hence, a detailed analysis of linguistic data which pertains to our topic will not be attempted here. However, a few notes on the diverse activities associated with magic seem to be in order at this point.

The following 'magical' activities are recorded in the Old Testament:

1.   Divination by hydromancy (by using or observing water), necromancy (summoning the spirits of the dead), and other

mechanical means.
2. Attempts to influence or control future events.
3. Attempts to summon or control God or gods, and to force them to obey man's wishes (an activity which presupposes that magic may override the power or will of the gods).
4. Performance of miracles (paranormal occurrences) as signs and portents for various purposes.
5. Interpretation of 'natural' phenomena as omens for the present, the future, and the will of God or the gods. This was highly developed and respected in Mesopotamia, where it was performed by various means, from liver analysis to astrology.
6. Warding off dangers to communities and individuals by verbal formulae and by practical means such as charms and amulets.
7. Causing harm to communities or individuals by manipulating destinies, casting spells, and so on. These were designed to further the aims of the initiator of the action, who rented the services of the performing magician. This category is the only one that can be named 'malevolent magic' or sorcery. As such it was forbidden by law in countries outside ancient Israel as well as in the Israelite community itself.

It is worth noting that the well-known folk figure of the male or female witch-naturopath is absent from the list. So is the Satan-worshipping witch, so prevalent in Western Europe and America during the years of the Witch Craze. The latter type of 'western' witch and the attitude towards it were probably fostered or encouraged by the emphatically negative attitudes of biblical literature towards self-styled witches and magicians. It is important, though, to remember that the figure of the Satan-loving witch, and the 'pact with the devil' legend, are completely absent from the Old Testament itself. Their earliest documented roots are to be found in extra-biblical Jewish literature of the Second Temple era and in the New Testament, where the figure of Satan is much more developed.

We have already said that although repeated and emphatic warnings forbade all magic in ancient Israel, some elements of it did enter the official cult or were not expelled altogether. Thus Joseph admits to practising hydromancy (Genesis 44), although this is done in Egypt and can be explained away by citing the need to conform to the behaviour of the Egyptians. Saul goes to seek the advice of the Endor medium in times of dire stress, although he himself has forbidden the practice and eliminated its practitioners earlier on (1 Samuel 28). Attempts to control God are of course unthinkable but the prophets, from Abraham (Genesis 18) onwards, try to summon and to influence him. Many personages, especially the pre-classical prophets from Moses onwards, perform miracles after the style of foreign wizards. Some priestly activities—such as the red heifer ceremony (Numbers 19), the cleansing ritual of skin diseases (Leviticus 13–14), the goat of Azazel (Leviticus 16), the consecration of Aaron's family, and many more—can be comprehended only in terms of preventive or thera-peutic magic. The same applies to Moses' making of the copper serpent in order to stop the plague of snakes (Numbers 21.9). In other words, whenever therapeutic, miraculous and affective properties associated with magic were taken over from other cultures and incorporated into Israelite religion, they became the tasks of the priest and prophet. The magician, as such, was not permitted to engage in his/her art, although members of the official cult were. In this way some practices were lifted out of their original pagan context—where, more often than not, they belonged to the religious sphere too—and legitimized by divorcing them from their origin and making them the property of the religious (and presumably orthodox) establishment. In Deuteronomy 18 the principle is explicitly pro-nounced. According to this passage a prophet will appear to each successive generation (vv. 15 onwards). Magic and magicians will be redundant (vv. 10-14), for the prophet will be the recipient of the only authoritative divine Word.

As we have already seen, women of ancient Israel were excluded from officiating in Yahweh's cult, and very few of them were recognized as prophetesses. Therefore women who practised magical arts risked condemnation, despite popular demand for their skills. This is not to say that women are the only persons accused of being magicians or witches; most legal injunctions name members of both sexes as culprits. However, men could and did perform some 'magical' tasks within the framework of accepted religion, while women were forbidden to do so.

On the following pages we shall examine a few biblical passages pertaining to women and magic. The first two are the narratives of Zipporah's action against the demon (?) who attacks her husband or son (Exodus 4.24-26), and of the anonymous medium from En-dor (1 Samuel 28). The third one deals with the magician prophetesses Ezekiel rages against (ch. 13). The next two sections briefly present the evidence of prophetic and legal sources in regards to magic in general, and female magic in particular.

b. *Zipporah (Exodus 4.24-26)*

At a lodging place on the way the Lord met him and sought to kill him. Then Zipporah took a flint and cut off her son's foreskin, and touched Moses' feet with it, and said, 'Surely you are a bridegroom of blood to me!' So he let him alone. Then it was that she said, 'You are a bridegroom of blood', because of the circumcision.[2]

This peculiar passage, according to Noth,[3] is almost inexplicable. Why is God depicted as a local demon? What is the child's role here—is he circumcised? Or is Moses, who is the victim of the sudden attack, the one who is circumcised? The Hebrew text is ambiguous on this point. Clearly, the narrative is an aetiological story so ancient that its original context and aim were far from evident even to the narrator who inserted it within its present framework in the Hebrew Bible. However, a few points can be gleaned from it with certainty. In contradistinction to later Jewish tradition and to other biblical passages which deal with circumcision (Genesis 17, Joshua 5), here a woman performs the ceremony. Moreover, she does so spontaneously, not by way of fulfilling God's command; and she does so in the accepted ancient manner—with a piece of flint (Joshua 5.2). Possibly we have adult circumcision connected with marriage (or sexual maturity) here, which constitutes a departure from the biblical norm where adult circumcision—when prescribed—has no link with marriage or puberty.

It is important to note that Zipporah, according to the story, behaves like a (male) witch doctor or holy man. Moses is in mortal danger, and she performs the apotropaic act of expiation by offering to the god-demon a part of Moses' manhood. In this way she manages to fight the angry aggressor, to placate him, and to save her husband from an untimely death. By offering a part instead of the whole, she magically manages to avert the danger. Thus, her action falls into our category 6 above, that of warding off dangers to communities or individuals by utilizing technical means. The story, however, is too short and isolated to permit any far-reaching conclusions regarding the role women, or female magicians/witch doctors, played in circumcision in ancient Israel (or proto-Israel). Let us also remember that Zipporah is a foreigner; and that the Old Testament freely acknowledges the prowess of foreign magicians without necessarily condemning them or explaining the authority for their actions.

c. *The medium of En-dor (1 Samuel 28)*

The story of Saul and the 'woman of a familiar spirit' (1 Samuel 28.7, NEB) from En-dor vividly illustrates the ambivalent Israelite attitude to this type of magic (spiritualism, or inquiring of the dead about the future) in particular, and magic in general. On the one hand, the profession is abolished and its practitioners persecuted even by King Saul himself (v. 3). On the other hand, the effectiveness of the practice as a means for predicting the future or God's will concerning it—especially when all other efforts of establishing contact with him such as consulting dreams, the Urim, and the prophets (v. 6) fail—is recognized as being beyond dispute. The Hebrew idiom itself—the woman is called *ba'alat 'ôb*, 'mistress of the spirits'—indicates that she is proficient in her craft. It is worth noting that Saul asks specifically for a woman practitioner, although other biblical passages show that persons of both sexes took up this vocation. In all the other passages these professionals are called *'ôbôt*, 'spirits' = 'raisers of spirits', and no technical details are supplied. This makes our passage unique and worthy of analysis.

After Saul's servants have found the woman medium, the king demands of her: 'Tell me my fortunes by consulting the dead' (v. 8). Then he goes one step further and asks for Samuel's spirit by name (vv. 8, 11-12). The woman complies after she has been promised personal immunity from punishment. It is a measure of her specific talent, or perhaps intelligence, that she actually recognizes Saul very early on, despite his attempt at concealment.

Although we are not told how the woman goes about her task, it seems that Samuel's apparition, once provoked by her into appearing, is visible to her only. Otherwise, why should Saul ask, by way of verification, for a description of the dead prophet? The woman's answer, 'I see a ghostly form . . . like an old man coming up, wrapped in a cloak' (vv. 12-13), depicts Samuel's ghost in conventional physical terms, as if his spirit still dwells within a living physical structure or has assumed such a form for the appearance. Once Saul is convinced of Samuel's identification, the woman's role is almost over. Although it is not at all certain that anybody but her can actually perceive the apparition, the king and prophet converse without her mediation. That is, even though Saul cannot see Samuel he can hear and recognize his voice. Conversely, the ghost (Samuel) can 'see', 'hear', and recognize the king; and is compelled—because it has been 'raised' by the medium—to answer Saul's questions.

The message Samuel's ghost delivers (vv. 16-19) is one of doom, of personal and national catastrophe. Saul is overcome with grief and fatigue (vv. 20 onwards). Characteristically neither the king, nor his attendants and the medium herself, doubt the validity of the message. It contains, as Samuel says, an authentic divine decision. Indeed, within one day it has come true (1 Samuel 31).

When defining the woman's role, the following points should be taken into account. She is an established professional who is well known for her particular skill. Like the two 'wise' women associated with Joab (1 Samuel 14 and 20), she is anonymous. Again like these two, she is not a travelling saleswoman; when one requires her services, one comes to her. The services of both classes of expert, 'wise' women and mediums alike, possibly had to be paid for (although the text remains mute concerning this detail). And, to conclude the analogy, at times of stress or emergency notables (Joab) and kings (Saul, David) turned to these women and the institutions they represented for counsel and guidance.

The medium's task is to establish contact between a particular ghost and a living inquirer. It is not clear how she manages to do so. Apparently she has the power to summon the ghost temporarily to the land of the living, even when this is done against the ghost's will. Once she is successful and the ghost's identity is established, she steps aside and lets the two parties conduct their business directly. However, she remains on the spot as long as the interview is in progress. Once it is over, she becomes active again—she deals with its after-effects on her clients (vv. 21 onwards).

The story is the only one of its kind in the Old Testament. Unlike other biblical trends and opinions of the First Temple era, it presupposes a 'real' ghostly existence after death. Hence, it is difficult to use it as a typical example of spiritualistic procedures in biblical times. As we have no other instances apart from the general warnings against the practice, this is all the material we have to go by. If the medium from En-dor is to be deemed a representative of her kind, her courage (for she performs for Saul despite the danger to her person), competence, and compassion (after the event, for she feeds the king who has previously persecuted her and her colleagues)—all these recommend her as well as her colleagues as worthy practitioners of their peculiar skill.

d. *Magician prophetesses (Ezekiel 13)*

Ezekiel rages against male false prophets who mislead the people (13.1 onwards), and threatens them with severe punishment (vv. 8-16). Then he turns to another, special class of false prophets, with whom he has a particular quarrel. This is the class of magician prophetesses. Ezekiel accuses these women of using mechanical aids, undoubtedly acquired in Babylonia,[4] for predicting fates and individual human destinies. The activity is quite common as far as non-Israelite magicians and witches are concerned. They were expected to reveal future destinies, for they supposedly had recourse to divine or parasensory knowledge. Ezekiel's anger stems from the conviction that these efforts are not inspired by the God of Israel. On the contrary: they are attempts to reveal what he wishes to hide or to disclose at an appropriate later date. As such, Ezekiel judges them to be an illegitimate activity in terms of Israelite religion. Moreover, these attempts do not necessarily produce valid results. Still, they cause damage for they are uttered as, and believed to be, authoritative and divinely inspired messages. This, contends Ezekiel, is a religious offence for a number of reasons. God chooses when to reveal his intentions, and should not be forced by pagan means to do so prematurely. Magician prophetesses have no place within his faith. No truth has been revealed to them and ordered to be passed on to their clients. Furthermore, they possess no power to influence or to change destinies.

According to some translators and commentators, the magician prophetesses were in fact guilty of practising black magic—that is, of attempting to influence rather than predict people's fates. This does not seem warranted by the text, for such an accusation would constitute a blunt admission of the effectiveness of the magician prophetesses—whereas, according to Ezekiel, they are totally ineffective. The women's chief sin does not stem from their skill, for it produces no truthful or reliable results. Rather, it is their proud pretence that their words are divinely inspired and the false belief they inspire in those who seek their counsel that God cannot tolerate. The fate of the false prophetesses is inevitable. Their aids will be taken away; their authority will be undermined by the non-fulfilment of their prophecies; and God will see to their punishment and downfall.

Interestingly enough, Ezekiel levels the specific accusation of magical prophecy against women only. His description of their practices suggests first-hand knowledge. Although he never admits the validity of their power, his rage is witness to these women's popularity and influence. Otherwise, why should he bother to attack them so vehemently? It appears that this profession evolved as a specifically female one among the Israelite exiles in Babylonia in Ezekiel's time. The practitioners, whose services could be hired (v. 19), were engaged for predicting people's fates. They used certain items of clothing or aids made of cloth in order to acquire the data sought (vv. 18, 20-21). They enjoyed a measure of popular fame, which necessitated a prophetic intervention by Ezekiel. This profile of a typically female magical occupation, of limited scope and a technical nature, has no equivalent in biblical literature. It does, however, correspond to elements of Babylonian practice within the same field.[5]

e. *Warnings of classical prophets against magic and witchcraft*

A cursory glance at the prophets' views concerning various categories of magic, from divination and necromancy to astrology and through a whole gamut of occult activities in between (cf. Deuteronomy 18; 2 Kings 21.6 = 2 Chronicles 33.6; and Jeremiah 27.9 for catalogues of magical activities) reveals the following:

1. Magic is either associated with foreign, pagan belief systems or with false prophecy within Israel itself. In both cases it is condemned in the strongest possible terms.
2. When associated with pagan beliefs, magical procedures are often described in a way that demonstrates first hand knowledge (Isaiah 2.6; 8.19; 47.9-15; Ezekiel 21.26-28; Micah 5.11). The Israelites are accused of adopting these procedures. Sometimes magic is defined as the equivalent of harlotry (Nahum 3.4; and cf. 2 Kings 9.22, about Jezebel) for it is conceived of as closely related to fertility cults.
3. Passages which describe false prophecy in terms of magic, or condemn magic as false prophecy, are quite numerous (Jeremiah 27.9; 29.8; Ezekiel 12.24; 13; Micah 3.6-7; Zechariah

10.2). The objection to magic in these passages appears to be derived from two claims: the illegitimacy of technical and mechanical means employed by the magician prophets, as opposed to Yahweh's direct word that is delivered to the true prophet; and the foreign origin of these means.

4. Most passages are directed at practitioners and alleged practitioners of both sexes, not specifically at women (excluding Ezekiel 13, discussed in [d] above; and Nahum 3.4, where the 'sex' is dictated by the metaphorical description of Nineveh as a wanton woman).

5. The repeated warnings uttered by prophets of the First and Second Temple eras alike prove that magic, witchcraft and sorcery were vital and widely popular throughout Old Testament times. Therefore they had to be continuously fought against.

f. *Magic, witchcraft, and sorcery in the Law*

Admonitions against magical practices in the Law (Exodus 22.18; Leviticus 19.31; 20.6; 26.27; Deuteronomy 18.10-14) exhibit the same views found in the words of the prophets. The objections stem from the afore-mentioned reasons: the pagan, non-native origin of magic (Exodus, Leviticus, Deuteronomy); and its association with false prophecy (Deuteronomy). There is no agreement, though, as to the punishment for magicians and witches. Exodus 22.18 relates specifically to female witches and prescribes a death penalty for them. The NEB renders the verse thus, 'You shall not allow a witch to live'. By so doing it widens the scope of the injunction to include witches of both sexes. This makes sense, for why should female witches receive a treatment different from that of their male counterparts? The Hebrew text, however, has $m^e ka\check{s}\check{s}\bar{e}p\hat{a}$, 'female witch', only. It does not specify how the female witch is to be executed. Leviticus 20.27 prescribes death by stoning for mediums and diviners of both sexes. Deuteronomy 18 forbids magic, but does not prescribe the punishment it entails. The text may indicate, albeit vaguely, excommunication ('Let no one be found among you who . . . ', v. 10) for soothsayers, sorcerers, diviners, and their like.

g. *Summary*

Magic and witchcraft, practised by males or females, is totally rejected by most Old Testament passages, be they narrative, poetic, legal, or prophetic—on the grounds of their foreign provenance and association with false prophecy.

The need for recurrent objections, together with the existence of many linguistic terms employed to denote magical activities, point to the vitality and popularity of magic in Israelite culture and sub-culture throughout biblical times.

By and large, women are not described as having a monopoly of the profession. Perhaps, as we learn from 1 Samuel 28 and Ezekiel 13, they did practise some branches of it more than males did. Otherwise, members of both sexes are included in the negative attitude displayed by the religious establishment to magic of all sorts.

Chapter 7

FEMALE PROSTITUTION

a. *Secular prostitution and sacred (cult) 'prostitution'*

The Old Testament knows of two types of prostitution: secular prostitution and cult prostitution. The two institutions are conceived of as similar, for they both involve a business transaction of a sexual commodity. Nevertheless, the Old Testament does recognize that there are certain differences between the two. The first type is related to women only; the second to persons of both sexes. The first is a morally inferior occupation, but indulgence in it is not a criminal offence and is tolerated within the fabric of society as long as the woman involved is not married. When she is, she is not only a prostitute but an adulteress as well, and should be put to death (cf. Genesis 38.24). The second, however, is rejected on moral and religious grounds, and totally prohibited. Passages in the Law (Deuteronomy 23.18), in the prophets (Hosea 1–3; 14.14; Jeremiah 2 and elsewhere; Ezekiel 23 and elsewhere), and in historiographical material (Numbers 25.1 onwards; 1 Kings 14.24; 15.12; 22.47; 2 Kings 23.7) amply illustrate how extensively practised were pagan fertility rites in ancient Israel throughout the First Temple era; how necessary it was to fight them; and how difficult they were to uproot. Members of the religious establishment felt that this foreign threat had to be eradicated. Repeated warnings and admonitions were made with zest and zeal. One of the means employed was the presentation of hierodules—considered professional temple officials whose services were essential for society and regulated by custom and law in neighbouring cultures—as common prostitutes. Thus, although Hebrew possesses two distinct terms for 'harlot' and 'hierodule', *zônâ* and *qādēš/qᵉdēšâ* (= 'a hallowed one', male or female) respectively, the two are often used interchangeably; or the first term substituted in narrative and prophetic writings for the more appropriate second. Tamar is referred to as a prostitute (Genesis 38.15, 24) but also as a hierodule (vv. 21, 22); the reader may speculate whether she claims to be the one or the other.[1] The Law is usually more precise. It employs the specific term 'hierodule' when prohibiting the practice, although the verb describing the activities involved is derived from the root *znh*, which is the base for the form *zônâ* = 'prostitute'; and which has come to denote also 'leave, turn aside' (from God).[2] The prophets use the term *zônâ* and related lexemes for female practitioners of fertility rites and their deeds. So does the Book of Proverbs in its exhortations against the Foreign Woman (Chapter 3, section g above). A woman who betrays her husband's trust is called a prostitute too, since she has 'turned away' from her lawful spouse. This is especially true in the case of the extended metaphor which depicts the relationship between God and Israel as that of a faithless bride or wife and a faithful loving husband, which is much employed by Hosea, Jeremiah, and Ezekiel.

For the reasons delineated above, biblical evidence of sacred prostitution should be regarded as tendentious and unreliable. Hence, it is excluded from the present discussion. Our concern here will be with 'common', secular prostitution. We shall limit ourselves to narrative material—the stories of Rahab, Solomon's celebrated judgment, and Tamar—and attempt to extract from them some information concerning the social standing and circumstances of the women involved.

b. *Rahab (Joshua 2)*

Rahab hides Joshua's spies in her house in Jericho and helps them escape from the king of the town, thus incurring a grave personal risk. She does so out of faith and a shrewd sense of political foresight, for she is sure that the Israelites will manage to conquer the city (vv. 9 onwards). In return she asks to be spared, together with her immediate family, when the day of victory comes (vv. 12-13). Her request is honoured later, while all other inhabitants of the city are put to death and their possessions are confiscated (Joshua 6.23-25). Rahab's family then joins the Israelite community (6.25), and is never mentioned again in the Old Testament. The New Testament places her alongside Tamar (Matthew 1.3) and Ruth (1.6) in the lineage of King David and, ultimately, of Jesus. She is said (Matthew 1.5) to be the wife of Salma (mentioned in Ruth 4.20, and also as Salmon in the next verse) and the mother of Boaz. Thus she is considered as worthy a foreign woman as the other two matriarchs, Tamar and Ruth. So much so that her assimilation into Israel was complete and that, by virtue of her loving grace, she was chosen to be one of the mothers of the great Messianic chain.

What can be gleaned from the story about Rahab's standing in her original non-Israelite community? She has her own house, which makes her a woman of substance. Her house is in the wall of the city (2.15), but this does not necessarily refer to her poverty; it may reflect her lowly social status rather than her material worth. She is unmarried and acts as protectress for her entire family, male and female alike. She conducts herself well. The text depicts her as a shrewd and courageous woman who successfully defies her king and his men and shows initiative and a strong instinct for survival—one who is intelligent, well spoken, and far-sighted. Is this the portrait of a common prostitute, barely tolerated by society as a professional who caters to base needs? Hardly, one would think. Her actions bear a strong resemblance to those of other great biblical women who save themselves, together with other members of the community, in times of danger (cf. Chapter 3 above).

Is it possible that, despite the explicit mention of her vocation (*zônâ*), Rahab is no common prostitute? Some commentators, including Rashi, explain that she was a food seller (from Hebrew *māzôn* = 'food'), not a harlot. Some modern commentators even substantiate this claim by referring to the Akkadian root *zanānu* B = 'feed', 'take care of one's needs'.[3] However, there is no trace of a similar verbal or nominal usage within Hebrew itself. The regular Hebrew root which indicates 'to feed' (*zwn*) is formulated slightly differently from the Akkadian one. Thus no basis in linguistic data can be found for the 'positive' interpretation of Rahab's occupation .

It is obvious that this interpretation is designed to resolve a psychological and literary difficulty, for how can such a great lady be a prostitute? The text itself shows no tendency to whitewash her. On the contrary: it repeatedly states that Rahab is known as a prostitute. Thus the harlot understands what the king of the city does not—that Israelite victory is imminent and inevitable. This element of irony enhances the impact of the tale. Its exclusion through whitewashing Rahab's vocation would have detracted from the dramatic and ironic properties of the story.

On the other hand, it is true that the story does glorify Rahab somewhat. She is a traitor who betrays her own community to strangers but, of course, nothing negative is said about this matter. Her character, as reflected in the story, is without blemish. Therefore it might be concluded either that Rahab is not a representative example of her profession, or that the Old Testament recognizes that prostitutes can be intelligent and perceptive. Nor can anything be learnt about the profession itself from the tale, for no reference is made to Rahab's vocation apart from the brief remarks that acknowledge it. Perhaps the biblical narrator found it unnecessary to expound on the subject because he assumed that it was self-understood.

c. *King Solomon's judgment (1 Kings 3.16-28)*

This celebrated instance of Solomon's wisdom and psychological insight—the identification of a true biological mother by threatening to have the disputed baby cut in half—bears the imprint of a folk tale. The analogical folkloristic element lies outside the scope of the present inquiry, which will deal with the two contestants only. Although the story is motivated by the wish to exalt Solomon, some details gleaned from it illuminate the life and social circumstances of the two prostitutes (Hebrew *zônôt*).

The two women are anonymous, presumably because they are treated as incidental to the main theme (the glorification of Solomon's wisdom) and hence their names are not important enough to be preserved, stated, or invented. They share a communal household, with no male patron or protector and no servants in attendance (v. 17). They seem to be poor, and are mutually helpful until the crisis occurs (vv. 17-18). Their maternal instincts are unaffected by their occupation: the one who loses her baby steals the other one's so as to compensate herself for the loss (v. 20); the second, the biological mother, would rather give her son up than see him killed by being cut in half (v. 26). An important lesson to be derived from the tale is that true maternal feelings—an extremely important thing for the preservation of social continuity—may exist even in the bosom of the lowliest woman. Hence the happy end: the true mother retains her child. Another important feature is that the women—isolated, unprotected, virtually outcasts—have access to the king himself and the right to appeal to him for judgment.

To summarize: The two prostitutes live together. They are probably poor and socially isolated. Nevertheless, their profession does not prevent them from appealing to the king himself for judgment. They are socially inferior, but legally equal, to their fellows. Finally, they display maternal instincts similar to those of other (decent) women.

d. *Tamar and Judah (Genesis 38)*

Tamar pretends to be a prostitute (or sacred prostitute) so that she can have a child by Judah, who has failed to marry her off to his third remaining son. In this way she wants to preserve the name of her late husband (Judah's eldest son), and to be released from the intolerable state of a widow in waiting. Her plot is bound to succeed because she acts not for personal pleasure or profit, but for a sacred aim—the continuation of her dead husband's line according to the custom of levirate marriage.

The story contains several details about prostitution and prostitutes. A prostitute hangs out in public places, where she waits for customers or solicits them (v. 14; cf. also the behaviour of the Foreign Woman, Proverbs 7.10-12). She covers her face, so that she is recognized for what she is by her attire (vv. 14-15, perhaps also Proverbs 7.10). Her services are enjoyed even by the Patriarch himself—only after his wife is dead and properly mourned for, to be sure (v. 12). The transaction between the two is conducted like a proper business deal, with the price pre-arranged and agreed upon by the two parties (v. 17). This act reflects Judah's eagerness as well as the custom of leaving a pledge in lieu of payment. Judah is as good as his word—he intends to pay the debt and retrieve his personal possessions. Still, he is embarrassed by his own behaviour. He sends his friend to look for the 'prostitute' but, once she is not found, he quickly gives the search up for fear of being ridiculed (vv. 20-23). Finally, he pronounces a death sentence against Tamar when he thinks that she—an unreleased widow, whose status is equal to that of a wife's—has prostituted herself by committing adultery (v. 24). His order is retracted after he sees his identity markers and accepts the responsibility for his share of the action (vv. 25-26).

So, according to the story, a prostitute is recognizable by clothing and appearance. She determines her fee by bargaining with her client. She may accept a pledge in lieu of payment, and collect the debt later. Association with her is not forbidden but, because of the social stigma involved, is better carried out discreetly.

e. *Conclusions*

Sacred 'prostitution' (= the practice of fertility rites), which infil-
trated ancient Israel from neighbouring cultures, was roundly
condemned and forbidden by the religious establishments. Indulgence
in it was a certain offence which carried the death penalty. Secular or
'common' prostitution, which is described as a particularly feminine
occupation, was socially tolerated—in the sense that its practitioners
were not considered criminals. Nevertheless, as in the case of King
Solomon's story, prostitutes could easily become social outcasts.
However, despite their social inferiority, they enjoyed recourse to the
usual legal procedures which ancient Hebrew justice offered to all
citizens.

Several details about the institution and the practice of prostitution
can be found in the story of Tamar. The recurrent prophetic
metaphor which depicts Israel as a faithless wife and harlot supplies
other details. The story about Rahab, however, does not contain
much which illuminates Rahab's profession.

PART II

LITERARY PARADIGMS OF FEMALE TYPES AND BEHAVIOUR

Chapter 8

GENERAL CONSIDERATIONS

a. Quite a few stories about women in the Old Testament are cast in recurrent moulds. The portraits of female heroines are often drawn in such a fashion that one gets the impression that these extraordinary women are not defined as individuals but, to a large extent, as generalized representatives of their type. Therefore, a listener/reader could expect to find that several basic features would be shared by most or all figures of any particular type. These shared features define the figures as recognizable manifestations of the type(s) or concept(s) they supposedly dramatize. The identification of a type which informs a particular story through its affinities with literary conventions within other, similarly motivated stories, will therefore enhance our understanding of both the passage under discussion and its parallels.

The identification of models which recur in literary fiction is important for another reason as well. A story is evaluated not only for its ideological contents, or message, but also for its plot. Here the model obtainable for the action sequence of any literary type is doubly important: first, because similarity in plot is usually related to similarity in message; and secondly, because deviations from a regular action sequence constitute the unique character of a given story and create the differences which account for its identity. In other words, a model is helpful, both the author and the listener/reader of a narrative, because it supplies a skeletal frame of reference, the departures from which give a story its particular flavour. Therefore, the critic or reader should read a relevant passage closely; identify the type(s) of personality that it describes; define the literary model or convention it follows; and then pay careful attention to deviations, elaborations, and specific details which constitute departures from the basic structure. By observing both type model and plot model, together with their deviations, one can achieve more enjoyment and better comprehension of the text on two levels—that of infra-structure and ideas; and that of super-structure and plot. To illustrate this point: when we read the narratives in which Sarah features as a protagonist we note that she shares certain traits and circumstances with other women. Some of these traits are: Sarah's barrenness until a late age; her beauty; her husband's love for her; her incredulous reaction to the message about Isaac's birth; her nearly miraculous conception after many difficulties; and, finally, her becoming the mother of an important person. Several other stories in the Old Testament present women in a similar way, so it seems that Sarah is cast in a mould. Like Hagar, Leah, Rachel, and other biblical women, her description essentially follows a stereotyped depiction of the Hero's Mother. Thus, the definition of the literary model Sarah's figure belongs to contributes towards our understanding of stories about her. However, this definition requires some expansion.

To begin with, a model is perforce an abstraction of several similar stories, which means that single stories that belong to a model or are structured upon it need not display all the features that make up the model. Further, those same circumstances which Sarah does not share with her other colleagues (her laughter and domineering ways) contribute greatly towards making her into a plausible character—if not a historical one, for this is an entirely different matter. As we should remember, we are dealing with didactic literature that presents what it regards as history through the filters of its own needs and aspirations. Therefore, in reading the Sarah narratives, and any other narrative in which women play a central role, which is our business here, one should go through the following stages:

1. Identification—definition of the female model (or female type) which the story presents, in terms of both personality and action sequence.
2. Compilation of a list of the main features which constitute the type.
3. Identification of departures from the type or additions to it, and their functional significance within the story itself.
4. Identification of other Old Testament stories which belong to the same model, and their analysis in similar terms.

b. This procedure, in essence, is followed in the next chapters. No attempt is made to give a comprehensive account of all female types, or of conventional descriptions of women, which appear in biblical literature. Rather, I have chosen a number of recurrent stereotyped descriptions which seemed best suited for illustrating the usefulness of the 'literary model' approach. These are the Hero's Mother (Chapter 9); the Temptress (Chapter 10); the Foreign Woman (Chapter 11); and the Ancestress, the first woman (Chapter 12). A resumé of the Male Leader and Female Leader types has already been given above, Chapters 4 and 5, because no discussion of female authors and prophetesses could be undertaken without reference to the models underlying these vocations. Obviously, some women who have been discussed in Part I (like Deborah, Tamar and Rahab) as representatives of female institutions reappear in Part II, and their stories are discussed from a different angle. It is hoped that the two strands of analysis complement one another and that, taken together, they will enhance our understanding of the subject.

c. Before we embark on a detailed discussion of female types, a few observations of a general nature are called for. First, we must remember that all or most of the stories we shall be dealing with were invented, preserved, and/or written by male authors. This does not necessarily mean that the literary result is always biased. However, more often than not the literary creation under discussion does represent a male's viewpoint, his comprehension of the female psyche, his understanding of female motives and behaviour, and his male judgment of all these factors. This may prove to be an excellent source for learning about male comprehension of, and conventional emotive attitudes to, the female world. It is less helpful, though, for the understanding of the female figures themselves. Unless we can establish, in any given instance, that the relevant story may have been composed by a woman (Judges 5?; and see Chapter 4 above), one should not fail to note that the types, be they what they may, stem from a male-oriented viewpoint. An important didactic function these stories are likely to have exercised is the continuation of the existing (patriarchal) social order. And this order—need it be said?—is of the utmost significance for the men who composed the stories and told them.

Secondly, all the stereotypes to which we shall presently refer are of an ambivalent or dual nature. In the case of the Hero's Mother the duality almost always assumes the form of a reality/appearance contrast, or that of a heroine and her shadow (Sarah and Hagar, Rachel and Leah, and so on). The common theme of the Patriarch who has two wives, a wife and a concubine, or two wives and two concubines, undoubtedly is an important recurrent feature whose function is central to the type. Thus, this feature should not be treated as a reflection of social (polygamous) reality only, but also as a meaningful literary device whose significance should be evaluated. Deviations from the dual pattern (like any other deviations from a recurrent structure) merit special attention. In the case of the next two models, those of the Temptress and the Foreign Woman, the principle of duality is different. Here we shall encounter 'positive' and 'negative' representatives of the same basic type. The two versions share some basic features of circumstances and behaviour, but differ in motivation and conduct. The judgment passed by the authors on the figures they describe stems from these differences. Nevertheless, the similarity between the two types is considerable, so that a single basic structure seems to underlie both of them. Therefore, while reading each passage that is structured according to either one of the two paradigms ('Temptress' and 'Foreign Woman'), one should investigate why it belongs to the 'positive' or 'negative' variety. The Ancestress, though, is a full and round figure. Good and evil, innocence and experience, stupidity and wisdom—these and many more apparent contradictions merge in her character. The result is a complex figure which exhibits a stereotyped (male) conception of the female principle. The balance of 'positive' and 'negative' elements, the relative weight assigned to them, and the understanding of the final judgment (if any) passed upon womankind in Genesis 2.4b–3 is of special interest for the understanding of the passage.

Thirdly, it will be seen that there is a certain overlap between models. The history of any particular woman may be construed in terms of more than one model. A good—but by no means isolated—example is that of Ruth, whose figure can be interpreted in terms of three types—Hero's Mother ('positive'), Foreign Woman, and Temptress. The convergence of several types within the description of a single woman does not invalidate the usefulness of recognizing the types and employing them for literary criticism: we define types and separate them from one another in order to improve our comprehension of a text, whose author is under no obligation to adhere to one type only. On the contrary: he may combine types deliberately in order to enhance the appeal, or stress the message, of his tale. The significance of such combinations, when they occur, should not go unheeded.

Finally, almost all the tales we shall presently discuss depict the fate of women within the domestic sphere, or chiefly within that sphere. The tales deal with women as wives, mothers, daughters—in short, women within the family circle. It is probably no accident that most of the recurrent female types are described within this setting of domestic life, which was considered normative for a decent woman. On the other hand, several individuals who managed to transcend the usual female destiny to such an extent that they made their mark on their male dominated society are exceptions to the norm. When such women (Miriam, Deborah) acquire positions of influence they are often judged by standards applied to male public figures; and the type they represent (for instance, that of the Community Leader in the pre-monarchical era) is not a specifically female type but a replica of the relevant male counterpart. Nevertheless, a hint of criticism remains, as if to say that they should have stayed in their proper place.

Chapter 9

MOTHERS OF GREAT MEN (THE HERO'S MOTHER)

a. *The Matriarchs*

Women of consequence who appear in the Book of Genesis are, in their order of appearance: the Ancestress, Eve; Sarah and her handmaid Hagar; Lot's wife and daughters; Rebecca; Leah and Rachel; Zilpah and Bilhah, maids to Leah and Rachel respectively; Dinah, Jacob's daughter who is raped by Shechem and avenged by her brothers; Tamar, Judah's daughter-in-law who seduces her father-in-law; and Potiphar's wife, who tries to rape Joseph in Egypt.

For the moment, our discussion focuses upon those matriarchs who feature in the stories of Genesis as complementary pairs— namely, Sarah and her maid; the two pairs of sisters, Lot's daughters and Leah and Rachel; and the latters' two maids.

Within the framework of their patriarchal and polygamous society, these women had to live together as co-wives and competitors. However, their presentation as mirror images or shadows of each other, in the sense that each member of a given pair has certain properties which the other lacks but tries to obtain for herself, has literary reasons inasmuch as it reflects socio-psychological conditions. If combined into one person, each pair would have formed a complete and balanced personality. Each member of a pair dramatizes a concept of incomplete, often indecorous, womanhood. Because they are depicted in terms of two conflicting sides of the same female entity, the two women involved are doomed to an almost constant struggle from the beginning of their story until its end—unless the one can get rid of the other.

Sarah is Abraham's beloved and only wife. She is good-looking and a lady of property, but is old and cannot conceive. Hence, she gives her personal maid Hagar to her husband for the purpose of producing a male heir. Juridically, this son will be considered Sarah's own, and the problem of family continuity will be solved. So far Sarah has behaved prudently. In her kind of society an individual has no power if he/she is not protected by the family. Therefore, family continuity is a supreme value that ought to override matters of personal happiness or fulfilment. Nevertheless, once Hagar becomes pregnant, Sarah is incapable of accepting the consequences of her own decision.

Despite her social superiority and her husband's love, Sarah does not feel confident enought to face the new situation. Hagar, for her part, does not behave properly. While she is Sarah's legal subordinate, inferior to her in status (Hagar is a slave and a foreigner) and probably in beauty, she exploits her pregnancy to disobey her mistress. According to the first story which relates to the Sarah–Hagar conflict (Genesis 16), Abraham is emotionally and legally helpless. Despite the fact that Hagar carries his own child, he hardly becomes involved in the power struggle between the two women. Sarah cleverly causes Hagar to run away, so that now she is an escaping slave as well as a rebellious one. However, Hagar receives a divine revelation in the desert, and comes back. According to the second story (Genesis 21), the conflict does not occur until Sarah has given birth to Isaac. But even now that she has become a biological mother, she is not satisfied. She makes Abraham send Hagar and Ishmael, Abraham's first-born son, away so that her own son will be his father's sole heir. Fortunately her action, which should be condemned as cruel and selfish, fits in with God's intention to make Isaac the carrier of his promise to Abraham.

The portrayal of the two women (in both stories) carries a clear message. Each of them is insecure in her lot. Their chief aim in life is to become biological mothers; and for this aim they are prepared to sacrifice everything, including the interests of the family unit and Abraham's feelings. Sarah does not feel secure until she gets rid of her inferior rival altogether. The implication is that women cannot cooperate even when they share a common purpose, for they let personal ambition and competition supersede other, greater values.

Leah and Rachel are two sisters who are married to the same man (Jacob). Leah is neither good-looking nor beloved by her husband, but she enjoys the position of first and chief wife. She is older than her rival sister, but fertile. Rachel is good-looking and beloved by her husband, but is a second (chronologically) and secondary (status-wise) wife. She is younger, but barren. Again, neither one is satisfied with her lot. Rachel says she is dead unless she conceives (Genesis 30.1) and, like Sarah, gives her maid to her husband. When she finally gives birth to Joseph she explicitly states that one biological son is not enough (30.21) and later dies in childbirth. Leah, who stops conceiving after having produced four healthy sons (29.35), is still not satisfied: she gives her maid to Jacob, so that her status as biological mother can be enhanced by her becoming a legal/adoptive mother as well (30.9). The two sisters are forever locked in combat. They compete for status and for their husband's love (see the incident of the aphrodisiac plant, 30.14-16), but mainly for male children. One gets the impression that even Jacob's love is sought after not for its own sake, but as a means for begetting more male heirs. Within the world of these women, it is possible to achieve personal security only through an abundance of sons. Love is secondary to a personal need which goes far and beyond a 'natural' maternal urge, and which is never wholly fulfilled. Thus, despite the fact that they are sisters, they cannot develop any kind of mutual intimacy, and their whole being is wrapped up in the conflict. The interests of the family, which is the basic unit for communal and individual survival, do not enter into the picture.

On the other hand, when the family is threatened from the outside, then the sisters cooperate with each other. When Jacob convinces his wives that their father Laban has used up their bride-price instead of keeping it for the children, they agree to cooperate with him against their father (ch. 31). They do so not out of love—nothing about their emotions is recorded, apart from the rage they feel towards the father-grandfather who robs his own kind—but out of the wish to preserve their sons' inheritance. When they feel that continuity is threatened, here as well as when the family is about to encounter Esau (ch. 32), they unite. Otherwise, each values her and her sons' interests more than anything else. Therefore they can be reconciled only temporarily; once immediate dangers are overcome, conflict and competition return.

Lot's daughters do cooperate with one another, for they believe that they and their father are the last persons on earth and that the human race is in danger of extinction (ch. 19). The older, more dominant daughter initiates the action and convinces her sister (who is socially her inferior) to follow her example. They are prepared to break two taboos—respect for a parent and incest—in order to secure the birth of the all-important male heirs. It seems that, unless they were convinced of the gravity of the imagined danger, they would not have cooperated for the achievement of their important aim.

The female pairs (Sarah and Hagar; Lot's daughters) and double pairs (Leah and Rachel and the respective maidservants) are described, in each case, as mothers or hopeful mothers-to-be. Despite differences in personality, circumstances, and setting they all conform to one literary type. In fact, they all belong to the 'Matriarch' or 'Hero's Mother' type that is an integral part of every narrative which belongs to the 'Birth of the Hero' paradigm. The recurrent features of such a paradigm—and all or only several of these features might appear in any given Birth story—are as follows. The mother-to-be is barren until a relatively advanced age (Sarah, Rachel; also Rebecca, Genesis 25; Samson's mother, Judges 13; Samuel's mother, 1 Samuel 1; and others). She usually receives an ironic divine promise to assure her of an imminent change in her sad plight (Sarah, Hagar, Rebecca, Samson's mother, Samuel's mother). The woman competes with and is humiliated by a maidservant, sister, or co-wife (Sarah, Jacob's wives, Samuel's mother) who is usually inferior to the heroine from the aspect of social status or the husband's affection, or both. The competition is so strong that both women involved cannot control it, to the point that all other values, including the welfare of the family unit, are overshadowed by it. The women continue to quarrel and bicker until they conceive. They are unable to experience personal security, even though they might enjoy an elevated position within the family, unless they do. They cannot cooperate with one another unless an external danger has to be faced. The inferior woman at first seems to be the lucky one: she is the first to conceive and bear a son (Hagar, Leah, Rachel's maid, Hannah's rival co-wife). The son or sons born to the socially inferior women are, however, false heirs. Finally, there occurs the birth of the true heir, an event which brings fulfilment and at least a semblance of security to his biological mother.

The authors who made use of this literary paradigm and depicted the women involved according to it convey to us, from their male viewpoint, some sharply severe comments on female behaviour and the female psyche. The implications of such stories are that women cannot be friends even when they share an important common purpose, namely the continuity and preservation of the family unit. They are incapable of feeling personal security until they become biological mothers. Shortly after that happy event they start to plot and scheme in order to further their son's ends; and are again insecure as long as their rivals, and rivals' sons, stay within the same household. Even when they are sisters rivalry, jealousy, and insecurity are so great that any possibility of empathy or affection between sisters is excluded. Men are seen as different, much more mature socially. Abraham and Lot are economic rivals, and are hence forced to part company. They do so with the utmost decorum and with no hard feelings (Genesis 13). Later Abraham saves Lot from a military danger (ch. 14). The behaviour of these two men, whose conflicting economic interests are irreconcilable, nevertheless remains gallant and friendly. David and Jonathan are bosom friends, although they are both aware of their political rivalry: they manage to keep their emotions intact and to be of service to one another even when this is to their personal detriment (Jonathan saves David from his father Saul, 1 Samuel 19). Men are capable of chivalry and can be depended upon to notice broader issues (although, to be fair, even blood brothers might become bitter enemies—Cain and Abel, Jacob and Esau). The difference between female and male behaviour is that while men are capable of honourable conduct towards other men even when they are under an emotional stress, women let personal considerations supersede any decent relationship with members of their own sex. This is the verdict delivered, in passing, no doubt, for it is just one of the many facets in the stories about the Matriarchs, on woman's nature.

Here we might stop, chuckle, and murmur: There is very little that is new under the sun. Traditional opinions and conventions change very slowly. The characterization of the female as a battle-axe who is unable to get along with other women, especially where her menfolk (lovers, husbands, sons) are concerned, is as commonplace today as in the Book of Genesis. Many people regard such female behaviour as normative and inbred, almost 'natural' in the sense that it is inherently female.

It is refreshing, therefore, to find an implicit criticism of this stereotype of female social behaviour in the Book of Ruth. The subject of the book is, again, the birth of a male heir. In this case the newborn is King David's grandfather. The story exhibits many features which belong to the 'Birth of the Hero' paradigm. There are two women, Naomi and Ruth. Naomi, the mother-in-law, is older and therefore socially superior. Ruth is doubly inferior, for she is the daughter-in-law and a foreigner. They do not have any children— Naomi's are dead and she is too old to conceive, and Ruth has been childless until now. The plot is complicated further by the need to find a prospective father. This element, although it does not appear in most of the stories we have discussed, is indispensable to 'Birth' stories in which the female protagonist conforms to the 'Temptress' type (which is discussed in the next chapter). Ruth follows Naomi, feeds, comforts and obeys her. Then she acts according to Naomi's directives, seduces Boaz and manages to compromise him, so that he promises to marry her (ch. 3). The marriage takes place and a son is born (ch. 4). Legally, we learn, Naomi is spoken of as the baby's adoptive mother (4.16). This newly born male heir, and not the land Naomi has previously owned (4.3), is the best and only security as far as she is concerned. At this point Ruth remains in the wings, so to speak, as if she has relinquished any hold on her biological son in favour of her manipulative mother-in-law. And here comes the surprise. The neighbours say to Naomi that the heir will be a comfort to her for 'your daughter-in-law, who loves you ... is better to you than seven sons' (4.15)![1]

This is the one and only place in the Old Testament where the possibility of alternative female motives is put forth. The author seems to be saying to us that a woman is capable of acting out of devotion and selfless love for another woman. This constitutes a departure from the stereotyped portrayal of females which we have encountered in Genesis. However, the love is not mutual. Naomi is not presented as acting out of love for Ruth: she is dutiful and certainly correct in her dealings with her daughter-in-law, but uses her for her own ends—the recreation of Elimelech and his house. Ruth, on the other hand, is motivated not only by duty but also by personal love and loyalty to her mother-in-law. Despite the exceptional circumstances, Ruth's behaviour is presented as a feasible mode of conduct, one that should be emulated. The fact that Naomi and Ruth do not have to compete for a husband, because of Naomi's age and inability to conceive, is not important. It is important, though, that as a pair they are similar to the pairs of women which recur in the narratives of Genesis and elsewhere; but this pair, which could have been doomed to constant struggle, manages to avoid such conflict because Ruth's devotion excludes this kind of conduct. Further, we have seen that the real bone of contention is always the male heir, not the husband. If this does not happen here it is because Ruth puts her devotion to Naomi, and, thus, the interests of the family unit, above her own need to enjoy her new authority as a biological mother. Ruth has a secure and full personality which makes the battle unnecessary. Therefore she can afford to love another woman and act according to this love. In her case, then, the production of a male heir is not an exclusive motivating force. We shall return to Ruth's story in the next chapter (Chapter 10, section a).

To conclude: The type of matriarch which is described in terms of the 'Birth of the Hero' paradigm proves that love between women, in contradistinction to love between males, or male and female, is impossible. Ruth, however, shows us that two women of the same family can cooperate to their mutual benefit, while one of them even loves the other. These two biblical views are diametrically opposed to one another; and the pictures each draws of woman's social behaviour within certain conditions and circumstances are widely different. Ruth's case is a departure from the 'norm', which is reflected in the motivation and behaviour attributed to the 'Hero's Mother' type.

b. *The birth of Moses (Exodus 2.1-10)*

Men hardly feature in the story of Moses' birth. The nameless biological father (2.1; elsewhere, but not here, he is identified as Amram) and the legal-adoptive father (the Pharaoh in whose palace Moses grows up) remain in the background. Even Moses himself, the axis around which all action revolves, is only a pawn: he is a helpless baby who does not participate actively in the forward movement of the plot. The actual heroines are the three anonymous women who attend Moses: his biological mother; his sister who puts him into the Nile and later arranges for his feeding; and the adoptive mother, Pharaoh's daughter. Similarly, in the previous chapter, and within a separate story, the Hebrew midwives manage to disobey the Pharaoh and save the Hebrew children—while no such male attempt is reported!

The story is a concise legend—and legend it probably is, for it contains several legendary elements. The heroes are anonymous, and it remains for other Old Testament passages to fill in the gaps and supply them with names. The difficulties attending the birth of the future hero correspond to hardships recounted in similar birth stories within biblical literature and outside it. Leaving the infant to the mercy of the elements, especially water, is quite common in this type of tale: similar adventures befell Sargon the Great, king of Sumer and Akkad,[2] King Oedipus, and others. The act of salvation is performed by a person of royal blood—this, again, is a common theme. Giving the child a name which recalls the event of salvation is another regular feature of this type of birth story (although, in our case, the etymology for the name is erroneous folk etymology). What distinguishes the story from other representatives of its kind on the one hand, and from the stories of Genesis we have discussed above on the other hand, is the tripartite division of labour. This time the role of parenthood is not assigned to two persons, one a biological parent and the other a saving/adoptive parent, but to three persons— or, specifically, to three women.

Had the story been constructed differently, with two parent figures instead of three, would it have still been effective? From the point of view of literary plausibility, the biological mother might have success- fully executed the role now assigned to the sister. This would have made sense, especially since the mother's own services as wet nurse are soon required and called for, so that she comes back to the scene. Nevertheless, placing the sister in an intermediary position beween biological and adoptive mothers makes even more sense. After the apparent removal of the biological mother, her reinstatement and reunion with her child through her assumed role as paid nurse is made even more poignant, ironical, and miraculous through the activities of a third person. Thus it seems that the expansion of the dual motherhood pattern which recurs in Genesis into a tripartite scheme is psychologically effective.

It is virtually unimportant for our analysis whether the biblical account of Moses' birth is a historically authentic story, or indeed, whether it contains strong historical elements. Even if the sister did exist, and did carry out the activities that are attributed to her, our argument—that the story could have been structured upon the dual motherhood pattern, and that if it were not then there must have been a reason for the expansion of the model—still stands. In addition, the sister's figure and actions could have been minimized or dropped altogether, as fiction, historical fiction included, allows. On the other hand, the sister's role could have been invented, or exaggerated, because it serves a purpose which is central to the story.

So, we come back to our question. Why did the storyteller deviate from the conventional model suitable for the description of the 'Hero's Birth'? It is as if the author wanted to convey to us that the danger to the male heir and future hero, who is the pivotal centre of the tale, is so great that two mother figures cannot overcome it without additional support. Two mothers are not enough, and therefore three figures have to pool all their resources in order to succeed. The greater the danger for the infant, the greater the miracle of salvation; and both danger and salvation indicate that the destiny of the child on whom all this care and effort are bestowed will be extraordinary indeed. Thus, a 'matriarchal' theme is expanded so as to draw our attention to the idea that this new hero, Moses, whose birth legend we have just read, will be an even more significant person than previous heroes (Genesis). In other words, the change made in the structural pattern of the story serves a purpose: it points to the future eminence of the newborn male son. On the other hand, the expanded pattern does not enhance the role of the women involved, for now the act of salvation is divided into three parts instead of the previous two.

c. Mary and Elizabeth (Matthew 1.18-25; Luke 1.5-80 and 2.1-7)

How are Old Testament traditions of the Hero's Mother type reflected in the New Testament? Fortunately, the two versions of Jesus' birth story (in Matthew and in Luke) allow for a double comparison: the two New Testament stories can be compared to each other, then to Old Testament material pertaining to the same subject.

According to Matthew, Mary, a betrothed virgin, finds herself pregnant by the Holy Spirit (Matthew 1.18). Joseph is a good man: he wants to dissolve the marriage contract (in accordance with Old Testament law, Deuteronomy 22.19 onwards and Numbers 6) quietly in order not to shame Mary in public. From the beginning, then, difficult circumstances attend the Hero's Birth, although the difficulties are of a different kind from those of Old Testament narratives, as is the case in many birth stories of great biblical men. Here, of course, the miraculous element which enhances the significance of the birth is taken to the ultimate limit—the Holy Spirit itself is involved; and the element of difficulty is supplied not by the barrenness or advanced age of the mother, but by the apparent transgression of sexual mores by Mary, and the regular attitude towards women suspected of adultery. (As Joseph's behaviour shows, others might not have been as merciful as he was.)

In this story (Matthew 1) the adoptive or earthly father Joseph, not the mother, receives a divine revelation in dream form. God reveals to him, as he did to Abraham, that a son will be born, and that this son's destiny will be extraordinary. The difference between the Old Testament model (the promise to Abraham) and its New Testament counterpart (the promise to Joseph), is, nevertheless, considerable. Whereas Abraham is Isaac's biological father, Joseph is his son's legal or earthly father only; and this difference in circumstances entails a different kind of message. The revelation to Joseph has an important function: it helps to dispel Joseph's anxiety about Mary's pregnancy and cancels out his plan to dissolve the engagement. There is no mention in our source of a similar revelation to Mary herself. But, how else would she know of her baby's parentage? After reading the stories of Sarah, Hagar, Rebecca, Samson's mother, and Hannah, one expects Mary to experience such a revelation, which is an important structural part of the Hero's Birth story. In fact, although the element of revelation to the prospective mother is absent here, it appears in the birth account in Luke. Luke 1.26 onwards records a divine revelation to Mary through an angel, as in the case of Hagar and Samson's mother.

To return to the story in Matthew. Once Joseph is convinced of Mary's innocence and God's plan, the rest of the tale runs smoothly. He supplies Mary with legal protection by taking her home as a wife. He does not have intercourse with her until after the birth, so that the infant's exceptional parenthood cannot be disputed later. In due course Jesus is born and named by his earthly father. This, again, is modelled upon traditions associated with Abraham, who names his children himself. In the case of other births, the women and/or their friends determine the names of the newly born infants. It seems that the parallels to Abraham's traditions are not accidental—the author tells us in his implicit fashion that, like Abraham, Joseph is the 'father' of a totally new religious heritage.

The exceptional circumstances of Jesus' birth are expressed, then, through two main themes: the irregular masculine parenthood; and the difficulty caused by Joseph's conventionally righteous, although merciful, morality. Thus the dual element which informs many Old Testament tales of heroes' birth—double motherhood, biological and legal (or triple motherhood, as in the case of Moses)—is here transformed into dual fatherhood, divine and legal-earthly. Could we conclude that the story in Matthew is a change in an Old Testament traditional pattern? It seems that the specifically matriarchal model has here undergone a process of patriarchalization; alternatively, it has not been utilized at all, although we would have expected the author to utilize it. Therefore, Mary's role is dissimilar to that of the matriarchs in Genesis and elsewhere. She is nothing but a glorified vessel—a vessel for a most precious cargo, but still a vessel.

The story (or stories) in Luke 1.5–2.7 is (are) much richer in detail and more complicated in structure than the narrative in Matthew. Old Testament motifs, especially those recurrent in Genesis, are very much in evidence. Our task here will be to identify these motifs, to see how and when they are reworked and developed, and what intrinsic purposes they serve.

The story in Luke 1.5-80, much like that in Matthew, displays strong affinities with Old Testament traditions about Abraham. It seems that the author used tales about Isaac's birth as a model and point of departure for his own narrative. Another interesting feature is the juxtaposition of Elizabeth and Mary as a complementary pair. Unlike pairs of matriarchs in Genesis and elsewhere (Hannah and Peninnah, 1 Samuel 1), the two New Testament women are not presented as rivals: they are kinswomen (Luke 1.6), but not married to the same man. They are both destined to bear famous men, and the pregnancy of Elizabeth serves as a sign and omen for Mary's (1.36-37). Elizabeth is of priestly stock, married, old, and barren; Mary is a laywoman, betrothed but unmarried, young, and fertile. Thus Mary is socially inferior to her kinswoman. Structurally, the situation is analogous to that of Sarah and Hagar, Leah and Rachel, perhaps also Hannah and Peninnah. When Mary visits Elizabeth, the older woman is quick to admit, without bitterness or envy, that the son of the younger woman will be superior to her own son (1.39-45). This straightforward acceptance is an improvement on the bitter struggles embarked upon by various matriarchs in order to improve their sons' lot—it is an act of faith unadulterated by suspicion. However, the superiority of a younger son (or a son born to a socially inferior woman) is a common biblical motif designed to stress the idea that divine blessing is a matter of choice, not of birth and/or social status. Thus Isaac, Jacob, Judah, Joseph, Moses, Jephthah, Samuel, Saul, David, and Solomon all belong to the same tradition of younger sons who are superior to their elders. The inability of the mothers to accept the divine decision without bickering is an integral part of the Old Testament paradigm of the 'Hero's Mother'. By contrast, Elizabeth displays the highest level imaginable of unquestioning faith. Both she and Mary (like Naomi and Ruth) are presented as devoid of competition and intrigue in regard to each other as well as to their environment. Unlike some of their earlier counterparts, their acceptance of their respective fates is gracefully and serenely complete. In that sense they represent an improved female breed. The implication is that their children will follow their mothers' example and cooperate, in contrast to the children of Sarah, Leah, Rachel, and the handmaids who, like their mothers, valued their own personal aspirations more highly than the welfare of family or community.

The future sons of Elizabeth and Mary, like their mothers, are the beginning of a line that will be better and greater than that of their predecessors.

Both Elizabeth and Zechariah are devout, and belong to the priestly aristocracy (Luke 1.5-6). Hence they are inherently suitable for becoming the parents of an exceptional child. Like Sarah and Abraham, they are both advanced in years (1.7), a detail that enhances the improbability of conception and the miraculous eventuality of John's birth. Both Abraham and Zechariah receive a divine revelation concerning the imminent event. Abraham responds sceptically to the divine promise of an heir from Sarah, so much so that he would prefer Ishmael to be the recipient of the divine promise (Genesis 17.17-18). Zechariah employs similar logic (Luke 1.18) and refuses to accept the validity of the divine message (Luke 1.18). Whereas Abraham is not punished for his doubts, Zechariah is struck dumb by way of punishment for his disbelief (1.19-22). He remains in this condition until after the birth, and until he agrees to the name his wife has chosen for the baby (John, Hebrew *Yôḥānān* = 'God will show/has shown grace', 1.64). Thereupon he is seized by holy inspiration and utters a prophetic hymn of praise and gratitude (1.68-79), just like Hannah after Samuel's birth (1 Samuel 2.1-10). From the literary-functional aspect, Zechariah's punishment and subsequent inspiration serve to illuminate the theological concepts of obedience and total faith in Providence, undoubtedly the product of repeated contemplation of Abraham's traditions. Similar religious sentiments inform the literary treatment of Elizabeth's. Unlike Sarah, she does not laugh, although the circumstances of both are very much alike. Rather, her belief is so complete that she stays in seclusion throughout her pregnancy, so as to guard the grace bestowed upon her (1.23-24). On the other hand, she does not receive a direct divine revelation: in that she is like Sarah, but unlike other mothers of heroes to be (Hagar, Rebecca, Hannah). The hymn (1.46-55) which is attributed by many versions to Mary could syntactically refer to Elizabeth's alleged authorship as well. However, authorship of a hymn still does not indicate that its author has been graced by a divine revelation. This grace is reserved for Mary (1.26-38), Elizabeth's seemingly inferior but actually superior shadow. Within the Abraham traditions revelations are affected through God himself, an angel, angels, or 'men'; here the carrier of the promise is always the angel Gabriel (vv. 19, 26). Mary is believing almost from the start—a departure from Sarah's behaviour, and a token of her well-deserved chosen state. Her visit to Elizabeth (1.39 onwards) might be interpreted as a display of the tiniest doubt, but even this is quickly dispelled.

Now for the birth scenes themselves. That of John, with the neighbours in attendance, is reminiscent of Obed's birth in Ruth (ch. 4). The naming of the child by the mother follows a well attested Old Testament tradition (Leah, Rachel, Samson's mother, Hannah), but constitutes a departure from the Abraham stories (where Abraham himself names his children, Genesis 16.14, 21.3). Zechariah's consent for the name is required nonetheless. Can we surmise again that this signifies a degree of patriarchalization of an ancient female prerogative—the woman still makes the decision in such a matter but, unlike similar cases in the Old Testament, her choice has to be approved by the child's father? The delivery itself is smooth, with no danger to mother or child.

Mary's delivery (2.1-7) is depicted in different terms and constructed after another Old Testament model. By royal decree, Mary and Joseph have to leave Nazareth in order to be registered in Bethlehem, Joseph's native town (vv. 1-5). This serves to stress the descent of Joseph (the baby's legal father) from the House of King David, and links the story with the tales of Tamar and Ruth. As a result of this untimely homecoming Jesus, instead of being born in the comfort of home, is endangered: his mother undergoes the risk of travelling close to the time of confinement and, on their arrival, the couple do not manage to find any lodgings (vv. 6-7). The literary device employed is transparent—the greater the danger for mother and infant, the more miraculous the birth seems and the more glorious is the destiny of the child. Structurally, the manger the baby is put in is the equivalent of Moses' rush basket. In both cases the infant is under threat from the local king and the elements of nature, and in both he survives to become a unique prophet. As mentioned above, the apparent abandonment of the infant-hero is well attested in many 'Hero's Birth' stories. Here the motif is modified somewhat— the baby is not abandoned, but suffers a degree of discomfort and risk. A triple prophecy delivered by the shepherds (2.8-20), Simeon (2.21-35), and Anna (2.36-38) reinforces the promise of Jesus' destiny. The prophetic utterances are the structural equivalent of a revelation to both parents together (as in the birth story of Samson, Judges 13).

d. *Summary*

Old Testament stereotyped stories (especially in Genesis) depict matriarchs singly or in pairs. When paired off the women are described as bitter rivals who cannot get along and who, instead of cooperating, jealously compete with each other. Exceptions to this general rule occur in the stories of Lot's daughters, and of Naomi and Ruth.

The paired-off presentation of Elizabeth and Mary is constructed after that of Naomi and Ruth. Other affinities with Old Testament traditions are related to stories about Abraham and Moses. The older traditions are treated as models, to be drawn upon, developed and articulated according to the convictions and aims of New Testament authors. A characteristic feature of the New Testament narratives is the relatively larger role assigned to father figures within the framework of such 'Hero's Birth' legends.

Chapter 10

THE TWO SIDES OF THE TEMPTRESS

a. *The 'positive' Temptress: Tamar and Ruth*

Many links connect Tamar's story (Genesis 38) to that of Ruth. Both women belong to the female side of King David's lineage (cf. Chapter 5, section d above). The basic circumstances in which both heroines find themselves are similar—the loss of the husband is followed by an attempt to produce a male heir who will continue the dead husband's name and, incidentally, supply his mother with the security only a male child can bring. Both are young and helpless widows, presumably attractive. Both are foreigners, although, even in Ruth's case, the foreign origin is of secondary importance only. Both fulfil their lack of a husband/son by resorting to charade and seduction. Their sense of timing is excellent: they exploit a joyful occasion (harvest, shearing) in which the chosen male victim, the necessary agent for realizing the woman's ambition, is replete with food and wine, thus more susceptible to sexual blackmail. Both are successful in their venture. In both stories there are males who at first seem to act as the destitute woman's saviour, but then turn out to be false saviours— the brothers of Tamar's husband, who do not give her children, have the same structural function as Ruth's 'redeemer' (Ruth 4). Finally, both Tamar and Ruth are involved with a father figure, be he a patriarch or a head of clan.

The many similar features should not obscure the fact that the two stories differ from each other in several details. Boaz marries Ruth, while Judah never comes near Tamar after she cheats him into giving her what she is after. As if to compensate for this factor, Ruth—who gains a husband—has one child only (or, at least, only one 'important' child), while Tamar—who remains husbandless—produces twin boys. Naomi functions as Ruth's senior shadow figure, to the point that there is some confusion in regard to her status vis-à-vis Ruth and the infant towards the end of the book, where she is treated as the 'real' mother rather than the grandmother (Ruth 4.13-17).[1] Moreover, Naomi undoubtedly serves as the child's legal/adoptive mother, a motif which we have encountered (Chapter 9) in other matriarchal narratives. Tamar, on the other hand, is alone: she gets no help from a shadow figure. Ruth's change of fortune is somehow tied up with the 'redemption' of Naomi's land (Ruth 4.1-10); this element is completely absent from Tamar's story.

Despite these differences, and the difference in scope, for the story of Ruth is so much longer, the two tales share one overall pattern of structure. A relatively young woman becomes, through no fault of her own apart from, perhaps, a touch of temporary barrenness, a childless widow. After she despairs of any other means of salvation she decides to take the initiative herself, and to resolve the situation which is intolerable from her point of view. In other words, she sets out to fill the lack she suffers from. The plot deals with the movement of her venture towards its satisfactory conclusion.[2] The woman's weapon is her sexuality. She chooses her victim with an eye to his social standing, and exploits his male vanity as well as his weakness for drinking. She compromises the male to such an extent that he must either admit the justice of her claim (Judah) or marry her (Boaz), or both. The woman's sense of time and place, together with her sexual charms, determines the inevitability of the outcome. In short, despite the differences (which ensure that the stories will be accepted as two separate literary pieces, each unique in its own right) the figures of both Tamar and Ruth undoubtedly conform to one basic stereotype, the Temptress who beguiles prominent but gullible males and subordinates them to her needs.

On the face of it, we might have expected the biblical storytellers to condemn women like Tamar and Ruth or, at least, to record a certain degree of dissatisfaction with their conduct. Disregarding sexual mores, abusing male trust, stepping outside one's social boundaries—these are a few of the hypothetical accusations that the authors could have levelled, implicitly or explicitly, against them. However, this does not happen in either story. Judah's admission that Tamar behaved more righteously than he did (Genesis 38.26) apparently expresses the author's opinion. Nevertheless, the positive judgment passed on Tamar's character and behaviour is not unquali-fied. Judah does not marry her, as if to say that the manner she chose for changing her circumstances tainted her somewhat. Ruth's figure is presented in an even better light than Tamar's. Throughout the book she is depicted as a paragon of virtue: even the temptation scene (ch. 3) develops from her obedience to Naomi and does not stem out of her own initiative. In short, the reader gets the impression that deeds attributed to these mothers of great men are recounted with relish rather than with an intention to moralize. They celebrate the matriarch's achievement to such an extent that the dubious means she employs are considered tokens of her resourcefulness and determination. The question is: What are the features in each story that enable the authors to rise above conventional morality and record the exploits of the Temptress without censure?

The answer pertains more to the motivation ascribed to the female protagonists than to the character traits, action or conduct attributed to them. Tamar and Ruth (and Naomi, who at various times fulfils various functions—she is Ruth's dependent as well as prime-mover and superego; in addition, she is chief beneficiary of the younger woman's actions) are motivated neither by pleasure-seeking nor by financial or social ambitions. On the contrary: the chief motive attributed to them is the desire to produce a male heir for their deceased husbands. This is regarded as a worthy, even admirable, motive. While it is recognized that personal salvation for a destitute woman can be achieved through wifehood and motherhood only, the women are presented as if this consideration were of secondary significance and not the chief reason for their actions. Furthermore, in prostituting themselves (an element which is more pronounced in Tamar's story), the women run an enormous risk. They know that if their plan fails society may reject, and even persecute, them for their attempt to ensure an orderly functioning of that same society through the production of suitable heirs. This kind of motivation and the extreme actions it requires is approved of, even admired. Women who risk whatever little social status they have, and possibly their lives, in order to perpetuate the continuity of Judahite leader stock display a rare kind of courage. Therefore, and despite the fact that they are foreigners, the authors who record their tales are on their side.

b. Lot's daughters (Genesis 19.31-36)

Lot's daughters conform to two types: that of the paired-off matriarchs (Sarah and Hagar, Leah and Rachel, Zilpah and Bilhah, Hannah and Peninnah, Ruth and Naomi); and that of the Temptress. The use of these two models, which are complementary but also contradictory, within the same story creates a structural tension. This duality and the tension it generates were caused by the transmission process this particular legend has undergone. As we shall see, certain views were probably advanced in the original version of the story, but others were insinuated once it was lifted out of its original context and inserted into its present place within the biblical text.

The two daughters, who remain nameless, function as a cooperative team, much in the way Ruth and Naomi do. One is older, thus socially superior and, appropriately, the initiator of the action; the other is younger and obeys her sister, as befits her inferior status. They commit incest in order to produce a male heir, for they believe that they and their father are the only human survivors of the Sodom and Gomorrah catastrophe. If judged by the yardstick used for the evaluation of Tamar's and Ruth's deeds, Lot's daughters behave in an exemplary fashion, according to their assessment of the situation that the future of all humankind is at stake. If the transgressions of Tamar and Ruth are justified, those of Lot's daughters should be justified as well. Perhaps even more so, because the situation, as they see it, is urgent. They are, of course, wrong in the assumption that the fate of the world now hangs upon their initiative; however, they act in good faith. Indeed, like Tamar and Ruth, they achieve success. They become the mothers of heroes: their sons (like those of Sarah, Hagar, and other matriarchs) found nations which are Israel's neighbours and are politically significant, one way or the other, throughout the First Temple era.

So far we have dealt with the 'matriarchal' elements in the story of Lot's daughters. Let us now examine the elements introduced from the 'Temptress' paradigm. The male victim is a biological father, which goes beyond the mere father figure (father-in-law or an older, influential relative) encountered in the stories of Tamar and Ruth. Tamar and Ruth exploit the fact that their male target has drunk, and therefore may be more manageable; Lot's daughters go one step further by actually making their father drink so as to ensure his befuddled cooperation. As we have seen, cheating the male whose awareness has been weakened by drink is an important ingredient of the Temptress paradigm. Once the male is weakened, Lot's daughters use their sexuality and seduce their father. As is dictated by their motivation, the daughters are not promiscuous: their interest in incestuous relations is limited to the preservation of mankind. Once they think that they have done their duty, they stop. One feels like asking: are they very different from Tamar and Ruth? They are certainly guided by the exact same motive! Why, then, is their story told mockingly, as if they were 'negative' temptresses? And why does not the author/editor of the passage (as it now stands) treat them with respect?

A number of possible answers have to be considered. First, in distinction from Tamar's and Ruth's plight, the basic premise from which Lot's daughters act is erroneous. The danger to all mankind is imaginary, and their assumption that the future fate of humanity is in their hands is arrogant—and ridiculous. This stupid error of judgment on their part, this impatience to wait and see how God, who has previously guided their own and their father's escape, will instruct them, marks them as misguided women rather than heroines. If this, however, is the case, why were they successful, and why were they allowed to become mothers of heroes and great nations?

A second possible answer is associated with the author's point of view. He might have felt that the strife for a male heir, although a positive value in itself, does not and should not justify a transgression of the basic Oedipal taboo.

Yet a third argument is again linked to the author rather than the subject matter of the story. Lot and his daughters are related to Israel, but still foreigners. Lot chose to part with Abraham and to strike out on his own (Genesis 13.1-12). Thus he and his descendants are not included in the divine promise of land and national blessing delivered to Abraham and his immediate family; and they deserve contempt for their ancestor's shortsighted, stupid decision. Unlike Tamar and Ruth, Lot's daughters do not link their personal destiny with that of the Israelite community. Hence, the writer does not feel bound to justify or excuse their actions.

The best and most plausible explanation is probably that supplied by Gunkel's theory concerning the provenance of the story.[3] According to him, this tale of the birth of Moab and Ammon may have originally belonged to the non-Israelite native traditions of these two neighbouring nations. As such, the story was transmitted with a relish similar to that displayed by the Judahite stories of Tamar and Ruth, which use the same basic paradigm. Incest is not prohibited as far as pagan gods or founding fathers of pagan nations are concerned, even though it is out of bounds for mere mortals. The mythologies of Canaan, Phoenicia, Mesopotamia, Egypt, Greece, and many others abound in examples of incestuous relationships. In the original version of the story incest was perhaps introduced as a positive element. By implication, the father figures Tamar and Ruth seduce are genteel reflexions of the ancient model, where the male enlisted for the production of a son is the biological father (or another close blood relative) of the Temptress. Be that as it may, when the foreign aetiological legend was incorporated into the cycle of Hebrew patriarchal narratives its original meaning was distorted. When lifted out of its cultural context the glorification of the ancestresses and their resourcefulness gave way to the contempt which stemmed from Israelite chauvinism and local patriotism. Israel's cousin nations were now ridiculed, and their mothers presented as incestuous fools and 'negative' Temptresses. Thus two components of an intricate pattern—the error and the incest—are emphasized in order to shift the female characters from the 'positive' to the 'negative' end of the scale of morality and value judgment.

c. *Potiphar's wife (Genesis 39) and the Foreign Woman (Proverbs 1–9)*

The features which are attributed to Potiphar's wife are totally different from those ascribed to Tamar, Ruth, and Lot's daughters. She represents another kind of Temptress, the 'negative' kind. The list of differences between the two sub-types can be summarized as follows.

1. Potiphar's wife is a disloyal married woman, not a destitute widow. Her passion for Joseph brands her as a potential adulteress even before she attempts to realize her desire.
2. She is motivated by passion and pleasure, not by the lofty ambition of securing a son and heir.
3. Her attempt is not successful, whereas the other Temptresses always manage to achieve the aim they have set out for themselves.
4. She is rather blunt and forceful. Instead of acting covertly and decorously, thus manipulating the male victim into complying with her wishes, she tries to convince him by using plain talk, then physical action. When this fails she tries to cover her tracks by lying, and accuses Joseph of an attempted rape.
5. She inflicts damage upon the man involved. This contrasts with the outcome of the 'positive' Temptress's action, whereby the man seduced gains a son (although this son may legally be considered as the heir of a dead relative, not of his biological father).

In short, the 'positive' Temptress, whatever her personal gain may be, in effect contributes towards the preservation of the existing social order. Her action reinstates a dead man's claim to his rightful place within clan and community and may even, as in Ruth's case, save his property from passing outside the immediate family. On the other hand, the so called 'negative' Temptress, as exemplified by the figure of Potiphar's wife, is characterized by a total disregard for the social order, a disregard which, if not checked, can ultimately endanger the very fabric of this order. A man's wife should know her place: if she is disloyal, she should be exposed and punished. Sexual politics is indeed used by both types of Temptress, but it is done in different ways and, most important, for different ends. The main issue is whether the Temptress's action benefits society, for within the society we are dealing with the individual must protect the social framework without which he/she is defenceless. Hence, self-fulfilment must be subordinated to the higher value of social order.

The Foreign Woman (Proverbs 1–9; cf. Chapter 3, section g above) is yet another example of a 'negative' Temptress. She shares quite a few traits with Potiphar's wife, and some additional features complete her portrait. Like all the other temptresses mentioned, 'positive' and 'negative' alike, she is a foreigner. She is a married woman who takes advantage of her husband's periodical absences, and indulges in adulterous activities. Her two chief weapons are her sexual charms and rhetorical skills. She states her business clearly and forcefully. Her motivation, though, is dissimilar to that of the other temptresses: it stems from passion (like Potiphar's wife), as well as the practice of fertility rites. This last feature is unique to her. Succumbing to her charms endangers the fabric of society, as well as the life and well-being of the individual. Therefore, she should be identified and avoided. In short, both Potiphar's wife and the Foreign Woman belong to the 'negative' Temptress type. The differences (or additions, in the case of the Foreign Woman) define each of them as belonging to a sub-type of their kind.

d. *Samson's women (Judges 14–16)*

Samson gets married twice, and both wives bring him bad luck. The anonymous first wife (chs. 14–15), who may exemplify a special kind of marriage, whereby the bride remains at her father's house, as well as Delilah (ch. 16) are both foreign—they are Philistines. They utilize sexual persuasion and verbal skills for the purpose of extracting from Samson either the meaning of his riddles (the first wife), or the source of his unique strength (Delilah). In so doing they cause grave damage to Samson, who in spite of his strength, intellect, and divine inspiration is like putty in their hands. Ultimately they bring destruction not only upon Samson's head but also upon their own and their countrymen's, for Samson's revenge in both cases is terribly effective. In other words, these women endanger the society in which they live to the point of physical destruction.

The features listed so far are those common to the 'negative' Temptresses described in the previous section and to Samson's wives. Some differences, though, are very much in evidence. Samson's wives are no adulteresses—even the first one, who at some point is given by her father to another man (Judges 15.1 onwards), cannot be accused of wilful adultery.[3] Furthermore, the motives for their behaviour are not hedonistic ones. On the contrary: they act out of loyalty to their native community—their family and Philistine society. It so happens that there is a conflict of interests between their native community and their husband's. According to the author, however, a wife should adopt her husband's interests. In this case, then, each Philistine woman should have suppressed her native patriotism (there is a hint that financial gain and personal safety play their part in the choice the wives made!) by subjecting it to the husband's. A wife's loyalty, on the political as well as the domestic level, is a basic requirement for an orderly family life. Samson's wives, once married, should have transferred their loyalty to him, but failed to do so. Their failure endangers the social order. This, in the last analysis, is their worst crime, inasmuch as it is the weightiest argument against any 'negative' Temptress. Lack of matrimonial devotion might lead to anarchy and the demolition of the communal framework of which the family is the basic unit, and without whose protection individual members of the community cannot survive. This is borne out by the final outcome of the stories. The Philistine community suffers a great loss and Samson, who should have chosen more wisely, pays for his fatal and repeated mistake with his life.

e. Summary

Characteristic features of the 'positive' Temptress type are: She is a husbandless foreigner, motivated by the desire to produce male offspring; a seductress who uses sexuality for achieving her aims; and a successful manipulator of her chosen male victim. The 'negative' Temptress is a foreigner too. She is married and an adulteress; is motivated by lust and/or foreign fertility cult practices; has considerable rhetorical powers, as well as sexual charms; and is not always successful in her attempts to manipulate men. The similarities point to the fact that the two kinds of Temptress possibly belong to one basic prototype which for literary and ideological reasons was divided into 'positive' and 'negative' halves. Structurally, the two sub-types perhaps relate to one basic model.

Ruth, Tamar, and possibly Jael (who will be discussed in the next chapter) belong to the 'positive' paradigm, Potiphar's wife and the Foreign Woman to the 'negative' one. Lot's daughters have more in common with the former than with the latter. Samson's wives present a variation on the 'negative' type. They are not adulteresses, but allow former loyalties to override the loyalty they owe to their husband. Loyalty to the male spouse is placed by the author/editor of the Samson cycle above other loyalties. We are told that when two values are in conflict, the right one should be chosen and adhered to, with no regard to any other value; and that Samson's wives failed to make the right choice.

Chapter 11

FOREIGN WOMEN

a. *Old Testament attitudes towards foreign women and mixed marriages*

From the very beginning of Israelite history patriarchs, leaders, and simple folk took foreign (non-Hebrew) women for wives, concubines, and mistresses. Hagar was an Egyptian slave (Genesis 16.21 and 25.12). Apart from her Abraham had another foreign wife, Keturah (Genesis 25.1, 4; 1 Chronicles 1.32-33) whom he took after Sarah's death. Judith and Basemath, Esau's wives, were Hittite (Genesis 26.34). Bathshua, Judah's wife, was a Canaanite (Genesis 38.2, 12; 1 Chronicles 2.3). Tamar, Judah's daughter-in-law and the mother of his twin children Perez and Zerah, was probably a Canaanite as well (Genesis 38). Joseph married Asenath, an Egyptian woman and the daughter of an Egyptian high priest (Genesis 41.45, 50; 46.20). Moses' wife Zipporah was a Midianite (Exodus 2.21; 4.25; 18.2), and his second wife was a Cushite (Numbers 12.1). Genealogical lists in Chronicles record foreign wives and concubines within the accepted structure of Israelite tribal society. These women were Egyptian (1 Chronicles 4.8), Aramean (7.14), and of other ethnic origins. Jael was a Kenite (Judges 4–5). Samson's two wives were Philistine (Judges 14–16). Ruth, King David's ancestress, was a Moabite. Bathsheba, David's wife and Solomon's mother, was perhaps a foreigner; at any rate, her first husband Uriah was a Hittite. Absalom's mother was from Geshur (2 Samuel 3.3 and elsewhere). King Solomon used foreign marriages as a diplomatic tool to an even larger extent than his father had done—he married many foreign women of noble descent, the most notable of whom was Pharaoh's daughter (1 Kings 3.1; 7.8; 9.24; 11.1 onwards). His heir Rehoboam was the son of an Ammonite woman (1 Kings 14.21), although we might have expected the Egyptian lady to be the mother of the heir to the throne. Asa's mother Maacah was probably an Aramean (1 Kings 15.9); Jezebel (1 Kings 16.13 and elsewhere) and Athaliah (2 Kings 8.26; 11; and elsewhere), of Phoenician origins. Mixed marriages, especially with women of neighbouring nations, were so prevalent during the time of Ezra and Nehemiah that both leaders felt duty bound to fight this practice (Ezra 9–10; Nehemiah 13.23ff.).

In short, according to the biblical records, many foreign women— many more than foreign men—intermarried into ancient Israel. Many of them turned out to be mothers of great men. King David's personal ancestry and history, for instance, are spiked with foreign females—Lot's daughters, Tamar, Ruth, and his wives Bathsheba (?) and Maacah. How did Old Testament writers, in various times and places, regard this phenomenon of ethnic impurity? As we shall see, mixed marriages were either overlooked or objected to. The reasons for upholding either of the two diametrically opposed views were dictated by changes in the political circumstances of the community.

The patriarchal stories in Genesis stress, time and time again, that a foreign wife is inferior to and less desirable than a woman of the man's clan or ethnic-national group. Abraham (Genesis 24.3-8, 37-41) and Rebecca (27.46) insist on endogamy at least for the favourite son, the carrier of the divine promise. Ishmael is inferior because he was born to a woman of foreign descent and lowly status, and married outside the family. Esau's Hittite wives annoy Rebecca, and serve as an excuse for sending Jacob to her family so that he finds a wife for himself. The migrant family of Abraham refuses to inter-mingle with the Canaanite nations of their new country. Inter-marriages did occur, but were frowned upon or—in extreme cases— prevented by force. Thus Jacob and his sons refuse the importantly political liaison with Shechem when they reject Hamor's proposal to marry Dinah (Genesis 34). It is true that, in this instance, another weighty principle is at stake—Hamor of Shechem had raped Dinah before he asked for her hand, and her honour must be avenged. The girl herself is not consulted and the Shechemites' readiness to make amends by joining the Israelite community is exploited but not taken seriously. It seems, therefore, that the pretext of a sister's honour— although it is one of the reasons for attacking the city—is less significant then the reluctance to lose the clan's unique identity through intermarriage.

Once the self-confidence of the migrants grows, they begin to explore the benefits of intermarriage as a device for their cultural and political acceptance into their new environment. Prominent families set the trend, for they are more susceptible to fresh cultural influence and ethnic assimilation than other families. From the beginning of the monarchy the number of intermarriages increases, and exogamy is socially tolerated to the point where it inspires indifference rather than anxiety. This attitude prevails until well into the First Temple era. It is usually assumed that a foreign wife will join her husband's family and adapt to its cultural and religious customs. From the time of Hosea, however (second half of the eighth century BC), the tide turns once more. Some classical prophets—Hosea, Jeremiah, Ezekiel, Deutero-Isaiah—compare the nation of Israel to a foreign born and inferior slut (Ezekiel 16.45, for instance). Narrative sources from this period onwards contain strong indictments against intermarriages; and Wisdom literature (Proverbs 1–9) presents the danger of associating with foreign women of a certain type in vivid, perhaps too attractive, terms. A curious picture emerges: the main stream of Old Testament ideology views foreign women negatively. At the same time, royal persons as well as lesser dignitaries and ordinary people continue to intermarry. The wrath expressed by the prophets and the anger of the other literary sources could not change this until, during the Second Temple era, the situation became so bad that the cultural and religious identity of the community was threatened. Then, by the mid-fifth century BC, Ezra and Nehemiah struck an official blow against the practice and excommunicated families who refused to send their foreign members away (Ezra 9–10; Nehemiah 13).

Intermarriage is perfectly natural and politically expedient. Why, then, did it provoke persistent opposition—which, for hundreds of years, did not succeed in suppressing the phenomenon?

The Deuteronomistic view of 1 Kings 11 argues that King Solomon's chief shortcoming was not his unwise treatment of the Northern Israelite tribes, but his inclination (in his later years) to indulge and even to participate in the foreign cults practised by his wives. Women are very often typecast as inherently religious; and when such a woman marries into an Israelite family—especially when she is of noble birth and good education—she tends to stick to her original religion. Instead of embracing Israelite religion, as they should, such foreign wives cause their menfolk to deviate from the right path and follow their pagan ways. King Solomon's wives, Asa's mother, Jezebel, and Athaliah—to mention but a few illustrious foreign ladies—all behaved in the same manner; and Cozbi, the daughter of a Midianite chief, nearly managed to convert an Israelite (Numbers 25.15-18). Women are viewed as chief practitioners of fertility cults by Hosea (mainly in chs. 2–3), Ezekiel (ch. 8 and elsewhere), Jeremiah (9.19), and other prophets. Israelite women are accused of practising these rites too, but foreign women are regarded as the most fanatic adherents of the rites. This foreign religious influence must have been so great—probably because the beliefs and the practices it entailed seemed attractive, or culturally and diplomatically beneficial, to the Israelites and Judahites who adopted them—that they had to be continuously fought against.

Because foreign women were generally associated with fertility cults, they became associated with seduction, prostitution, and sexual disloyalty also. Even the best of them, those who were assimilated to the point that they became matriarchs and local or national heroines (and see section b below), are described as operating within the framework of sexual seduction. The associative chain which links foreign women with fertility cults, sexual promiscuity, and unscrupulous disloyalty is used many times by various prophets, from Hosea onwards, as a model for describing Israel's attitude towards God in terms of a relationship between a loving husband and his faithless, often foreign immoral wife.

Some prominent foreign women have already been discussed above, under headings pertaining to their sphere of influence (Part I—Jezebel, Asa's mother, Athaliah), or the literary model which informs their description (Part II—Tamar, Ruth, Rahab, and others). In order to avoid redundancy, the following remarks are confined to one particular aspect: What defines a given foreign woman as a positive or a negative character? Jael's case, which has hardly been touched upon so far, will be dealt with in greater detail than the other stories.

b. *The positive side:*
Tamar, Ruth, Rahab, and Jael

There are a few features which are shared by all four women, or by most of them. All of them are seductresses, amateur or professional: Tamar seduces Judah; Ruth does the same thing to Boaz; Rahab is a prostitute; and Jael, who puts Sisera in her own bed and hits him so that he 'fell between her legs' (Judges 5.27, according to the Hebrew text), probably used her charms as part of her apparent hospitality— sexual connotations are part and parcel of the story. Tamar and Ruth feature in the genealogy of King David and, according to a New Testament source (Matthew 1.5, where Ruth and Tamar are mentioned as well), so does Rahab. All three marry into the tribe of Judah and produce male children who turn out to be leaders. At first glance Jael seems to differ from her three colleagues for, as far as we know, she is childless. In addition, she is not a single woman who marries into the tribe of Judah. Jael is a married woman, the wife of Heber the Kenite. However, the Bible describes how the Kenites, originally a non-Israelite clan or tribe, were slowly assimilated into Judah. This process of assimilation was first geographical, then ethnic (Judges 1.16; 4.11, 17; 1 Samuel 15.6; 1 Chronicles 2.55). Indeed the foreign origin of the Kenites is noted, but no importance is attached to it because they cooperated with the tribe of Judah and were later incorporated into it.

Tamar and Ruth place the welfare of the family they have joined above their personal interest; Rahab and Jael prefer to serve the cause of the adopted community. By so doing, all four reap a personal reward as well. Their foreignness enhances the impact of their deeds, and their acceptance within their chosen community is assured.

By choosing this particular path, all four women incur grave risks to their person, and face these risks courageously. Tamar risks being burnt as an adulteress. Ruth leaves family, home, religion, and culture in order to accompany Naomi into a strange land and an alien cultural milieu. Rahab is in danger of being exposed as a traitor to her home town. Jael might have easily been overpowered by Sisera, a seasoned warrior who, even when exhausted, still possessed a presumably strong instinct for survival. All of them succeed because of their faith, and because they serve the right cause. It is no wonder, therefore, that their characters are judged to be extraordinarily righteous, and their contribution is acknowledged without any reserve. In short, when a foreign woman chooses to adopt Israelite (Judahite) society and religion, and her behaviour indicates that she is seriously committed to her new community, then her acceptance is guaranteed.

Tamar, Ruth, and Rahab have been discussed previously, and therefore no more will be said about them now; however, a few additional words about Jael seem to be in order. Unlike her three colleagues, Jael is a married woman. It even seems that she actually commits adultery with Sisera. The text (Judges 4–5) does not say so explicitly; nevertheless, various euphemisms and references to legs, beds, and so on impart broad sexual connotations. Because of her marital status, Jael's deeds could have been condemned by the biblical writers. However, she is not classified as a 'negative' foreign woman. In her case—as in that of Rahab's—political and military considerations which involve the community as a whole are placed above considerations of conventional morality. The narrator's viewpoint is encountered again and again: whenever two social principles come into conflict (in this case, sexual standards of an individual *versus* survival of the community), the Bible teaches that survival comes first. Similarly, during the Maccabean period, self-defence in times of emergency was defined as more important than the observing of the Sabbath. When everything else fails, then, even adulterous seduction is a legitimate means of eliminating an elusive enemy. In this instance Deborah's—and Barak's—considerable talents prove to be inadequate: the outcome of the battle is not decided until Sisera is killed, and this they do not manage to do. It is perhaps symbolical that Deborah and Jael have to combine their resources in order to defeat Sisera. At this point Barak disappears from the scene, and does not participate in the conclusion of the battle.

A sizable part of the poem (Judges 5) deals with the two heroines— Deborah and Jael—and with their victim Sisera. The juxtaposition of the two heroines is interesting. Deborah is a female community leader—prophetess, military strategist, poetess, and judge. However, her figure lacks sexuality and domesticity: the attribute *'ēšet lappîdôt*, which is applied to her name, can be understood either as 'wife of Lappidoth' (an individual about whom nothing else is known), or simply as 'a spirited woman'. The Hebrew term *'ēšet* lends itself to both renderings. The Jewish Sages, who speculated about Lappidoth, identified him with Barak, thus supplying Deborah with 'wifely' integrity and womanhood. This interpretation, as we have seen, is linguistically uncertain. It is informed by the extralinguistic opinion that a woman, even when she is active in the public sphere, should retain her distinctive duties and sexuality. Otherwise, she cannot hope to be either happy or completely successful. Deborah, despite the efforts of the commentators, is sadly lacking in these 'feminine' qualities. Therefore, a complementary figure is required. Jael, who is represented as Deborah's complement, spends her whole life inside the domestic framework. She uses hospitality—a traditional virtue— and sexuality as devices for winning the battle. Without her initiative the end might have been different—and yet, whatever she does could have been done by any ordinary woman, for she uses no weapon but her own self. Is there a note of censure in the way events are told, an implied criticism levelled at Deborah for her deficiency as a woman? Jael herself, at any rate, is typecast as a representative of a well-established intercultural tradition—that of a brave married or widowed woman who sacrifices, or seems to sacrifice, her virtue in order to save her people. Another (post-biblical) instance of the same type—

later in date and more refined in tone—is Judith, who kills Holophernes by using deceit and seduction (Judith 8–13).

c. *The negative side:*
Potiphar's wife, Samson's women, and the Foreign Woman of Proverbs

Potiphar's wife and Samson's women are temptresses of a dangerous kind: their behaviour has fatal consequences for their male victims and, sometimes, for their own selves (cf. Chapter 10, sections c and d above). They share quite a few formal traits. They are foreign and married. They are faithless—be it for reasons of sexual desire (Potiphar's wife), cult (the Foreign Woman), or loyalty to a previous community (Samson's Philistine wives). This is their biggest fault. When a woman marries, she should join her husband's community. Like Ruth, she should forsake all other loyalties in favour of her newly-found one. Otherwise, law and order within the community will be supplanted by anarchy. Instead, these foreign women remain loyal either to their own personal interests or to those of the paternal household. Therefore, the readers are warned, they and their like are unacceptable. The results of consorting with them and other women of the same type will invariably turn out to be calamitous. Thus Joseph goes to jail—an event which, ironically, serves to elevate him to a position much higher than the one he occupied in his master's household. Samson loses his strength and is blinded; when he regains his unique power he commits suicide, destroying many Philistines together with his own person. And the Foreign Woman of Proverbs, that clever female of loose morals, devious charms and deviant religious convictions, is fatal for her followers.

d. *Summary*

Foreign women were accepted into the Judahite/Israelite community if and when they were prepared to forsake their previous ethnic, cultural, and religious ties and to adopt the systems of values and beliefs prevalent in their new environment. When this basic condition was met, exogamic marriage was either permitted or else overlooked. When a woman continued to practise foreign ways even after her marriage, she and her children were disapproved of. The examples of Tamar, Ruth and Rahab show that whenever a foreign woman demonstrated that she valued the welfare of her chosen community above her own she was accepted without further reference to her origins.

Most of the stories about women of foreign descent focus on these women's sexuality, or powers of seduction. This places the description of most of them within literary paradigms which have been discussed earlier. Thus Tamar and Ruth are temptresses; Rahab a prostitute; the Foreign Woman of Proverbs a prostitute, sacred prostitute or simply an adulterous woman; and so forth. Therefore, it is impossible to delineate a stereotype which would efficiently define all or most members of this group. In most cases, the foreign origin of these women was judged to be secondary to the more important features which make up each character, or which determine what literary type it belongs to.

Chapter 12

THE ANCESTRESS—AN EXTENDED FEMALE METAPHOR
(Genesis 2.4b–3.24)

a. *The story of the First Man*

I find the story of the Garden an extremely difficult and frightening topic to discuss. It is one of the best known and most written about passages of the Old Testament. Most readers either view it as a cliché of male chauvinistic attitude, or as a justification for these same attitudes. It is well-nigh impossible to contemplate such an important literary opus objectively. One tends to read into it ideological conceptions and biased opinions. So much has been written about it, in ancient as well as in modern times, that an attempt to approach it afresh is doomed to failure almost from the outset. With these reservations in mind, I would like to advance a few tentative remarks concerning the contents and meaning of the passage.

Many people interpret the Garden story as a tale of human disgrace, of the fall of mankind from divine grace through the initiative taken by the first woman. If this is really the main theme or *leitmotif* of the story, it should contain a strong, one-dimensional, single-minded condemnation of the female species. As we shall presently see, this is not exactly the case. Although the first woman, spiritual mother of her sex and prototype of her daughters and sisters in successive generations, is roundly blamed for the expulsion from the Garden, she is not simply typecast as a foolish and villainous person, but characterized as a complex figure. The expulsion itself, although it entails a loss of comfort and deprivation of contact with the divine cosmic principle, is inevitable in terms of other details in the narrative, which are not directly linked to the woman's conduct. These details are built into the narrative from its very beginning, so that the woman's action—although it is of crucial importance for the outcome—does not generate this outcome exclusively. Furthermore, the rift between Creator and created is not only unavoidable, but also beneficial for mankind. The concept that man is a combination of earthly and divine elements is extremely important. Hence, the critic must trace this important theme throughout the story, and attempt to understand how the typification of the first female is related to it.

A cautionary note seems to be in order at this point. The present biblical narrative (the text of Genesis 2.4b–3.24) has a complex history. Partial parallels and corresponding motifs in other ancient Near Eastern literatures bear evidence of the fact that the questions— and some of the answers- the story deals with were treated in a similar fashion before the Genesis narrative was formed. Therefore, a certain amount of literary borrowing on the part of the Hebrew writers is to be expected. Several inner inconsistencies or redundancies (like, for instance, the two names *ḥawwâ* and *'iššâ*—of the first woman, each with its own folk etymology) are probably the result of the composite nature of the text. A lengthy and complex process of composition and transmission provides a fairly adequate explanation for apparent contradictions and discrepancies. However, once we choose to deal with the end product of the transmission process (the present text), historical considerations should be relegated to a secondary position while literary ones are given precedence over all others. The following remarks are limited to the literary aspect of the present text which—regardless of its composite nature and complex history—is treated as a unified work of literature, whose contents is motivated by a well-defined didactic-theological system.

According to Genesis 1 man and woman were created as a pair after all other creatures had come into existence. In Genesis 2.4b–3.24 the order is different: man is created first, then the Garden, plants, and animals. Woman is created from the man's rib almost as an afterthought. When we read the story we notice that it is constructed in such a way that each detail is significant, either for the plot or the ideological contents which underlie it. The author, it seems, does not wish to surprise the reader with sudden unforeseen twists of plot but to hint, at every single stage, at something that will unfold at a later stage. Thus the order in which the act of creation is told, together with the details attendant upon it, must be important. If the woman was created later than man, plant and beast—does this mean that, according to the writer, she is inferior to all three classes of beings? Or, following the principle according to which mankind, male and female, is created last in Genesis 1 because it is superior to all other forms of life—is woman superior, the pinnacle of divine creative activity? This second interpretation does not fit the context of the story as a whole: woman's secondary origin (from the man's rib) and her later conduct do not point in this direction. Whatever way we look at it, the order of creation does reflect the view that woman is inferior to her mate. This fact, however, does not sum up the attitude of the story as a whole; other, conflicting views are expressed in it as well. Neither does it imply that woman is of little or no significance, for she is the only partner suitable for the man. The reader's task is to examine the evidence of the text; and to assess the relative weight of the negative and positive traits attributed to the first female and, by extension, to the sex of which she is the archetype.

Let us return, for a moment, to the beginning of the passage. From the very start man is a polarized creature: he is fashioned out of earth, but is given a divine spirit (2.7). Thus man is a link between heaven and earth, an intermediary figure whose strength lies in his dual origin—but so does his weakness too. Can the two elements live within him harmoniously? Will the twain ever meet? If, broadly speaking, we equate 'earthly' with 'evil' (or 'insubordinate', 'negative', 'foolish', 'primitive,' 'chaotic', 'physical', 'unconscious') and 'divine' with 'good' (or 'obedient', 'positive', 'intelligent', 'articulate', 'organized', 'spiritual', 'conscious') then future conflict between the two aspects of his personality within, and between him and his God without, is unavoidable. When, at any particular instance, earth wins, man will remove himself—or be removed—away from his Creator. When spirit predominates, he will come closer to him. No permanent solution to this conflict can be arranged. Furthermore, the material used for fashioning man is earth (the significance, again, of the chronological order!), while the spirit is introduced as a second, perhaps secondary, element. Hence, earth is the most dominant element in man's makeup. In short, the separation of man from the divine element external to him is to be expected even before the female appears on the scene and supplies the immediate means for this separation, for man is more earthly than divine from the very first moment of his existence.

The eventual expulsion from the Garden is inevitable for other reasons too. God is portrayed as a rather benevolent, albeit tyrannical, male parent. He is a progenitor who is kind enough to give his child life, a cosy existence, and suitable playmates. In return he demands total obedience, and practises constant supervision over his child. The youngster is denied two basic liberties: the knowledge of good and evil, inherent to man but waiting to be converted into awareness (which is symbolized by the Tree, forbidden yet lovely to behold and flourishing in the middle of the Garden!); and the freedom of choice—between awareness and innocence, adulthood and eternal childhood. Like many authoritative parents, God secures the young generation's obedience by threats. This type of parental behaviour undoubtedly stems from the parent's anxiety that once the child matures and achieves awareness he/she will leave the parent's side. And what does a normal child do when subjected to this kind of parental pressure? He rebels. He wants to grow up and go out into the wide world beyond. He usually succeeds, even if the price required is the destruction of the parent. We expect the child to sever the metaphorical umbilical cord which links him to the parent so that a new relationship between the two will emerge. Otherwise, we think, the child will suffer emotional suffocation, or become a disturbed semi-adult. This separation of parent and child is a prerequisite for the maturation of the child. The price paid by the child is the loss of previous physical and emotional comfort. This loss is nonetheless compensated for by the possibility of entrance into a brave new world. The parent must adjust to the new situation. Can the expulsion from the Garden be avoided? Or, more important still, should it be? Should we hang on to our children, although we know that their emotional and spiritual growth will be inhibited if we insist on so doing? Modern psychology condemns domineering parents such as God, who uses a classical 'double bind' method—a combination of favours and threats, carrots and sticks—in order to tie his offspring to him. Whether we agree with this presentation of the celestial Father, or whether we see it as an unjust projection of human psychology onto the divine, this is the view presented in the passage. Moreover, the relationship between (divine) parent and (earthly-divine) child is depicted, from the start, as a disappointment for both sides: the parent is a distant one, and the child is bored with the parent and needs more company. This is why God creates the animals, but they fail to provide adequate company for man. Therefore, God creates woman.

b. *The story of the first woman—and mankind*

The First Woman—hence all women—is part of man, made out of his own flesh. Here too future conflict is present from the outset. The extraordinary Hebrew idiom which describes the female's function vis-à-vis her man, '*ēzer kᵉnegdô* = 'a helper against him' (Genesis 2.18, 20), is a contradiction in terms which depicts relations between the human sexes succinctly—and hints at the ambivalence of the attitudes toward womankind which are expressed in the biblical passage.

The implications of the basic notion—that woman was created out of Adam's rib while the latter was unconscious, or in a kind of trance—are manifold. Man is therefore always slightly weak and fuzzy in his dealings with women, which explains his consent to eating the fruit and calls for more caution on his part in the future. Woman is autonomous but belongs to man, and the two will always strive to be reunited. She is secondary, and twice removed from both divine spirit and earthly material. Hence she can act more decisively and devote less time and energy to hesitation and self-consuming inner struggles. This state of affairs accelerates the unfolding of the plot. The serpent approaches the woman, knowing not only that she would listen but also that she would understand that God has lied to his child in order to prevent the child from leaving him. Indeed, although God threatens that man will die on the day he eats from the forbidden tree, this never happens (2.16-17; 3.3). Woman is convinced by the serpent: she seizes the forbidden fruit, eats it (3.6), and makes her husband eat too. In so doing she commits an act of disobedience— but, under the tempting circumstances, is not this to be expected? And are the consequences of the act so terrible? Even God admits that after the eating all that differentiates him from mankind is his eternal existence, and therefore he hastens to expel the humans from the Garden before they eat from the Tree of Life too (3.22-24). In other words, by eating from the tree the woman has transformed herself and her man into near-replicas of the divine principle himself, so much so that he is afraid of their intelligence. Incidentally, this 'acquired' similarity to the Godhead is—according to the first story of creation in Genesis (1.1–2.4a)—bestowed upon mankind, male and female, from the very beginning—for they are created 'in God's image' (Genesis 1.26-27). In the Garden story, however, it is acquired through temptation, deceit, and disobedience.

If one draws up a profit and loss account setting out the consequences of the eating for the first human couple and their successors, and especially for the first woman and her sex, the following picture emerges. On the debit side, woman has caused her husband and herself to be separated from parent and birthplace; to be doomed to hard labour, misery, and eventual death; to strive throughout life to return to a past existence of innocence and the security inherent in the proximity of the divine. She brought upon herself the pain of childbearing and doomed herself to an ironic reversal of roles: man now subordinates her by way of punishment for her forwardness and initiative (2.17-19), contrary to the original state of affairs. There was no reason to insert the celebrated matriarchal saying of 2.24 ('That is why a man leaves his father and mother and is united to his wife, and the two become one flesh!') within the present patriarchally oriented story unless it reflected the idea that, to begin with, woman was the stronger and dominant partner; and that she forfeited this position by behaving badly. Man gained his dominance over woman not by his own strength, but because woman's punishment dictates that he sujugates her. The Ancestress's initiative, energy, and persuasiveness are endearing; on the other hand her disobedience, lack of responsibility and judgment, and her sly approach justify her punishment.

On the credit side: what has the human race gained? It gained the freedom to move and go to places unheard of before. It acquired self-awareness and an ability to exercise judgment and discretion. It chose to learn what good and evil meant, and how to recognize the gamut of shades that lie between these two poles. It gained sexual knowledge and an ability, hitherto dormant, to procreate. By eating from the tree it leapt irreversibly into maturity and civilization, for consciousness (symbolized by shame and the subsequent attempt at self-clothing, 3.7) is the cornerstone of culture and social order. Woman was the instigator of this process of human growth and struggle to lead an independent life, albeit one of hardship.

Is freedom so worthwhile that it should be snatched or pursued even when it entails loss of life (or longevity)? Is a state of knowledge preferable to a state of innocence, even when the former implies suffering and the latter comfort? Is painful maturity preferable to pleasant childhood? These and related questions are for each reader to decide according to his or her own personal convictions. The story itself presents these existential human predicaments without offering clear-cut answers. Only one of the problems raised receives a definitive answer. To the question, Why is man, even a truly religious man, always separated from his Maker?, the answer given is: From the very beginning of human history close proximity was inherently impossible on account of man's dual nature and the choice (the Tree) with which God burdened him and his woman companion.

Let us summarize. Women—every woman, every Eve—deserve to be managed by their men. They are resilient, obstinate, energetic, intelligent, shrewd, and enterprising—but also misguided, easily seduced, and morally inferior to their male mates. The hardship they suffer in giving birth is their own Ancestress's—and, by implication, their very own—fault. They are the mothers, initiators, and ultimate preservers of human culture as we (author and readers) know it. Indeed, woman is the primal source of trouble and pain for the entire human race—but she is the source of human learning, consciousness, and civilization as well.

c. *Genesis 2.4b–3.24: Echoes and Interpretations in the New Testament*

Although several women were closely associated with Jesus, who apparently held no prejudices against the female sex as such, women fare badly in the New Testament.

Here and there we do encounter women who functioned as public leaders or supporters of the new ideology, as also we find some who were bitter opponents of the emerging creed. They certainly played a considerable role in the establishment of new communities. Nevertheless, it is repeatedly stressed that their proper place and fundamental tasks are domestic. Pauline doctrine is adamant on this point. Passages like 1 Corinthians 11.14, 34; Galatians 4.4-7; Ephesians 5.22; and Colossians 3.18 reiterate the usual patriarchal ideas. A woman should be obedient to her husband. She should remain silent in public. If she wants to understand community affairs or spiritual matters, she should receive instruction from her husband at home. A woman can learn but not teach, so that her silence in public and inferior position vis-à-vis males are maintained.

The silence in public and domestic subjugation prescribed for women refer back to the story of the Garden and the curses upon woman that are contained in it. The rationale of ironic retribution— the reversal from persuasion to silence, from a domineering position to subordination—supplied an ideological base for these recommendations concerning appropriate female conduct. This element of 'justice' is already present in Genesis 3, where it serves as an explanation for an existing social order. In the Pauline passages the principle is taken one step further: it is presented not only as an explanation for a social phenomenon (as in Genesis), but also as a moral justification for this phenomenon. Similarly, in Genesis 3 childbearing is mentioned as a painful experience for women, caused by the Ancestress's transgression; in the New Testament this statement of fact, which traces the aetiology of birth pains, is accorded a new significance. Childbearing, as painful as it is, should be woman's occupational role in life; and through its dedicated practice she may achieve salvation for her soul.

An explicit formulation of views concerning women, their character, and role is to be found in 1 Timothy 2.9-15. Women should behave and dress modestly: good deeds are much more important than external appearance (vv. 9-10). A woman should be quiet and obedient (v. 11), never domineering (v. 12). Two reasons are supplied for these prescriptions: (i) Man was created first and woman second (v. 13), which expresses the relative importance of each partner; (ii) Man did not contemplate eating from the Tree, whereas woman did and sinned (v. 14). Henceforth, she should be closely watched so that she does not commit similar sins. Her salvation lies in patient faith and childbearing (v. 15).

These are the views attributed to St Paul. For the present purpose it matters little whether they are authentic Pauline teachings or not. Even if they are the product of a later hand which added them and ascribed them to the authority of Paul, they still reflect social mores that were prevalent in his time or slightly later. Besides, too many such passages appear in Paul's letters for all of them to be additions. The ideas concerning women—like others advanced by the great preacher—stem from Old Testament views which are further developed, and often given a new turn or direction. In the case of women, Pauline teachings reflect a tighter, more exclusive and moralistic system of values. The Old Testament does maintain that appearances are less important than faith and good deeds (Proverbs 31.30), and female finery is of no consequence (Isaiah 3); however, it does not forbid feminine finery *per se*. In contrast, early Christianity advocated the suppression of female finery in favour of modesty and devout behaviour. Female subordination, aetiologically explained in Genesis 2.4b–3.24 as the outcome of the Ancestress's action, is elevated to the level of religious value in the New Testament. And childbearing, woman's traditional and biological role, becomes a religiously endorsed sole function in life for every fertile female (see also 1 Peter 3).

According to Genesis 3, one of the direct consequences of the eating from the Tree was the discovery of human sexuality. Pauline doctrine advocated celibacy as the best condition for serving God without succumbing to earthly diversions, while marriage was viewed as a lesser need (1 Timothy 7). Sexuality in Genesis is not a sin or evil in itself: in Genesis 1.27 (the first creation story) it is a primary and inherent trait of humanity, and in Genesis 3 the discovery of sexuality is that of a divine secret withheld from man until woman snatches it. By contrast, Paul considers sexuality to be a wasteful diversion of energy and a hindrance to the real business of a true believer's life. Hence, he devalues sexuality. Eve, every woman, is the Temptress—a sensual, irresponsible, frivolous, sinful being. This rejection of sexuality, undoubtedly useful to the founders of the new creed, was extended to refer to the community as a whole. It is clear that within such a community women could not flourish, for they were looked upon as reincarnations of a base sexual principle which is either pagan or faithless. Only women who de-sexualized themselves—or were de-sexualized—by denouncing personal sexuality could aspire to influence, public respect, and saintliness. Christianity emphasized spirit over matter; eventually Mary's virginity was confirmed and the doctrine of the immaculate conception formulated, so as to remove all hint of 'earth' and 'flesh' and leave only the 'spirit' (cf. Genesis 2.7). Thus the conflict between earth (flesh) and spirit, inherent in man's nature, is brought to an end by the descent of the Son of man and the victory of the Spirit. Mary—in her turn—is regarded as the new, pure, de-physicalized Eve. This process of purification and spiritualization of the female principle lies, however, outside the literary and religio-historical scope of the present study.

Chapter 13

CONCLUSION

We have discussed two topics: a number of Old Testament institutions associated with women, and conventional patterns used for the literary description of several female types. The two topics overlap in places: a prophetess is described in certain set terms, much as a temptress, 'positive' or 'negative', is drawn with a conventional portrait in mind.

The picture that emerges is significant for the anthropological archaeology, or reconstruction, of Old Testament societies in general, and the status of women within these societies in particular.

Woman's proper realm, according to the Old Testament, is the family and domestic pursuits. The best and most useful way for her to express herself and achieve personal security is through bearing children, and especially male children. Many actions designed to achieve this aim, actions which in a different context would have been deemed immoral because of sexual taboos and social mores, are justified by the biblical writers. The principle of social preservation and continuity is, then, a supreme value in biblical society.

Woman is subordinate to man—not necessarily because she is less intelligent or less inspired than he is, but because she is considered irresponsible and in need of protection from herself.

These two prevalent views—that women's chief role is inside the (married) home, and that they should be placed under male surveillance—almost exclude the possibility of regular female participation in public affairs. Exceptions occur and are sometimes judged quite severely (Miriam). The top positions in Israelite society—the priesthood and active monarchical roles—were never open to women. Prophetesses, female writers, female orators, and female public leaders of other kinds are very few. Tribal society was probably kinder to them—some social institutions, like that of the 'wise' women, are linked to the old tribal order. From the early monarchy onwards, these institutions become extinct and even forgotten altogether. Deborah—again before the monarchy—was the only woman to achieve any degree of military prominence. It seems that women were excluded from the military professions too, in reality if not officially. Furthermore, even ladies of noble birth found it difficult to be acknowledged as public figures in their own right— whereas their sisters in Mesopotamian, Egyptian and Canaanite societies did occupy official positions. On the other hand, some occupations of a more technical nature (mourning, music, magic), which may lead to public prominence, were open to female and male practitioners alike. There is no doubt, however, that those professions were socially inferior to the ones closed to women.

The literary paradigms utilized or created for describing women and female behaviour vary. Nonetheless, a few shared characteristics inform all or most of them. These characteristics reflect the considered opinions of biblical (male) writers in regard to the Second Sex. According to them women are at their best and most efficient when they use traditional female weapons (= sexual charms) for achieving their goals, in the private as well as public sphere (Jael, Tamar, Ruth and others). They are not to be trusted because their personal ambitions may all too easily overshadow their judgement and social conscience (the Ancestress, Sarah, Hagar, Miriam, Potiphar's wife). Hence, they should not be allowed to govern (Jezebel, Athaliah, Miriam, and—to a lesser extent—Deborah). They may be intelligent, educated, enterprising, and attractive but are still considered as not mature enough, emotionally and morally, to occupy positions of power even when they want to do so. They might enjoy a queenly status within their own married home but only very few can aspire to, or manage, a public career. Apparently, as Israelite society became more and more institutionalized—especially since the founding of the monarchy—women became increasingly excluded from the public sphere on all levels, even the lower ones. The political establishment refused to accept them as equal participants in the business of government. The few exceptions, let us emphasize once more, make this state of affairs even more manifest.

Thus woman, the instigator of human civilization, finds herself unable to participate in the power struggles and decision-making that determine the shape of this same civilization. Instead, she is confined to a biological-social function which is extremely important for the continued existence of society, but is not significant politically. In short, she is to be—politically and socially, if not emotionally and biologically—a minor throughout her life, unless exceptional circumstances decree otherwise.

AFTERWORD: A PERSONAL NOTE

Earlier this summer I met an Australian woman, a self-declared feminist of the fairly militant type. She has heard about this book from a mutual friend and expressed interest in it. After I had described it in detail, she said:

> You know, the trouble with academic women who write about women is that they limit their efforts to the re-writing of history. The current trend is to transcribe history, 'he-story', into 'she-story'. I cannot comprehend what value this exercise holds for the cause of women. It affords yet another kind of socio-historical interpretation and is widely regarded as just that. This kind of work will be of no use to feminists because it is not radical or revolutionary enough, whereas outside feminist circles it will be regarded either as too radical, or else as of no interest.

At first I was taken aback, even offended; then I started to think. Was I really trying to re-write Old Testament narratives in female terms? This was not what I set out to do. Initially it seemed to me that certain areas of investigation linked with women have been either sadly neglected or else—in recent years—treated from biased viewpoints (be they feminist or male-oriented). I hoped to make a small contribution towards filling in the gaps. I could not, of course, be 'objective' about the material I was working with: being a female student of biblical literature and culture excludes this from the outset. Neither did I aspire to being 'objective': there is no reason or justification for masking one's personal convictions. On the other hand, these convictions—so I thought—should not be allowed to dominate the interpretation of the material or produce too many errors of judgment.

If to 're-write history' means to search for facts and factors that have been lost or suppressed through the long transmission of ancient Hebrew literature within the framework of patriarchal society, then this is probably what I attempted to do. Hopefully, a fairly clear picture did emerge. Women in biblical literature may have been respected as individuals, but as a class they undoubtedly were a Second Sex—second in importance, social standing, and civil rights. This, to my mind, is a basic premise which—at this stage of women's studies—needs no further verification. Much work is still to be done if a fuller history of Old Testament women and consequently, of Old Testament society as a whole (and throughout its various eras), is to be 're-written'. Women's studies, we are all aware, is a young field waiting to be explored.

This work is indeed 'not radical' in feminist terms, while it is perhaps too radical for readers who do not espouse the feminist cause. No apology will be made for that, because the literary material itself dictated the results of the investigation. As for the usefulness of this study: if it promotes a slightly better understanding of its topic, then its modest purpose will have been achieved.

NOTES

NOTE TO CHAPTER 1

1. A few Jewish priestesses are known from post-biblical inscriptions, however. Cf. S.J.D. Cohen, 'Women in the Synagogues in Antiquity'. A fuller treatment is now available in B.J. Brooten, *Women Leaders in the Ancient Synagogue*.

NOTES TO CHAPTER 2

1. For her name and identity see J. Gray, *I and II Kings*, pp. 347-48 n. 9.
2. W. Hallo, 'Women of Sumer', pp. 23-40.
3. *Ibid.*, p. 27.
4. H. Lewy, 'Nitoqris–Naqi'a', pp. 264-86.
5. For the meaning of Jezebel's name see H.J. Katzenstein, *The History of Tyre*, p. 146 n. 85.
6. Josephus, *Antiquities*, 8.13.1; also the Babylonian Talmud Sanh. 39.2; 102.2; Jerusalem Talmud Sanh. 10.2; 28.2.
7. Montgomery–Gehman, *The Books of Kings*, pp. 40-41; J. Gray, *I and II Kings*, pp. 371ff.
8. M. Weinfeld, *Deuteronomy and the Deuteronomic School*, pp. 19-20, 24.
9. Josephus, *Against Apion*, 1.18.
10. Hallo, 'Women in Sumer', pp. 29-30.
11. Herodotus, *Histories*, 2.44 (p. 147 of the Penguin English edition).
12. W.B. Fleming, *The History of Tyre*, pp. 146-47; Katzenstein, *The History of Tyre*, p. 151 n. 113.
13. N. Avigad, 'The Seal of Jezebel', pp. 274-76.
14. For a different view of Jezebel's role see G. Fohrer, *Elia*, p. 56.
15. H.J. Katzenstein, 'Who Were the Parents of Athaliah?', p. 197.

NOTES TO CHAPTER 3

1. U. Cassuto, 'Il palazzo di Baal', pp. 285-86.

2. P.R. Ackroyd, *Samuel*, 195.
3. *Ibid.*
4. R.B.Y. Scott, *Proverbs*, pp. xv-lii; W. McKane, *Proverbs*, pp. 51-208; R.N. Whybray, *Wisdom in Proverbs*, pp. 11-32; Whybray, *The Book of Proverbs*, pp. 3-9.
5. Whybray, *The Book of Proverbs*, pp. 9-11.
6. *Ibid.*, pp. 26, 30, 31.
7. Cf. Whybray, *The Book of Proverbs*, and McKane, *Proverbs*, for discussion of the passage.
8. For a short survey and bibliography see R.J. Clifford, 'Proverbs IX', pp. 298-306.
9. Whybray, *Wisdom in Proverbs*, pp. 13-14.
10. Not 'adulteress', as Whybray has it in his commentary *ad loc.*
11. *ANET*, p. 420.
12. Whybray, *The Book of Proverbs*, pp. 55-56.

NOTES TO CHAPTER 4

1. M. Pope, *Song of Songs*, pp. 40-89. But see the recent treatment of F. Landy, *Paradoxes of Paradise*.
2. C. Rabin, 'The Song of Songs and Tamil Poetry', pp. 205-19.
3. For a detailed bibliography see Pope, *The Song of Songs*.
4. C.D. Ginsburg, *The Song of Songs and Coheleth*, pp. 4ff. Ginsburg's opinion is discussed in Pope, *The Song of Songs*, pp. 136-41.
5. Pusin in Pope, *The Song of Songs*, pp. 133-34.
6. Exodus 14 contains a prose account of the same event, which does not agree with the poem on certain points. For the question of the relationship between the two variants see B.S. Childs, *Exodus, ad loc.*
7. The Book of Deuteronomy is written as a long speech delivered to the people by Moses before his death; and Jewish tradition identifies him as the author of the whole Torah (excluding the verses dealing with his demise). The poetic compositions (to be distinguished from other literary genres) attributed to him are Exodus 15, Deuteronomy 32, and Deuteronomy 33.

NOTES TO CHAPTER 5

1. M. Noth, *Exodus*, p. 222.
2. The interested reader may consult the entry 'Mari', by A. Malamat, in the *Encyclopedia Judaica*, vol. 11, pp. 987-89. The entry includes a representative bibliography up to 1971.
3. J. Gray, *Kings*, p. 726.
4. Montgomery–Gehman, *Kings*, p. 525.

5. See, for example, *Yalkut Shimeoni*; cf. Josephus, *Antiquities*, 10.4.2.
6. R.J. Coggins, *Ezra and Nehemiah*, p. 96.
7. *Ibid.*, p. 97.
8. M. Noth, *Exodus*, pp. 122-23.
9. *Ibid.*, p. 123.

NOTES TO CHAPTER 6

1. See R.C. Thompson, *Semitic Magic*.
2. Exodus 4.24-26; quoted from Noth, *Exodus*, p. 48.
3. *Ibid.*, p. 50.
4. Cf. W. Zimmerli, *Ezechiel*, pp. 281-99.
5. Cf. Zimmerli, *op. cit.*

NOTES TO CHAPTER 7

1. G.M. Astour, 'Tamar the Hierodule', pp. 185-96.
2. BDB, pp. 275-76.
3. CAD, Z, pp. 43ff. The root appears in texts from the Babylonian period onwards, especially in religious and cultic contexts.

NOTES TO CHAPTER 9

1. Cf. also B. Green, 'The Plot of the Biblical Story of Ruth', pp. 55-68; Brenner, 'Naomi and Ruth'.
2. *ANET*, p. 19.

NOTES TO CHAPTER 10

1. Cf. Brenner, 'Naomi and Ruth'.
2. Cf. Sasson, *Ruth*, pp. 191ff.
3. Gunkel, *Genesis, ad loc.* (Genesis 19).

SELECT BIBLIOGRAPHY

Abbot, N., 'Pre-Islamic Arab Queens', *AJSL* 58 (1941), 1-22.

Ackroyd, P.R., *The First Book of Samuel* (CB), Cambridge: CUP, 1971.

Astour, M.C., 'Tamar the Hierodule: An Essay in the Method of Vestigial Motifs', *JBL* 85 (1966), 185-196.

Avigad, N. 'The Seal of Jezebel', *IEJ* 14 (1964), 274-276.

Batto, B.F., *Studies on Women at Mari*, Baltimore and London: Johns Hopkins, 1974.

Bardèche, M., *Histoire des femmes*, vol. 1, Paris: Stock, 1968.

Basserman, L., *The Oldest Profession: A History of Prostitution* (tr. J. Clengh), New York: Stein and Day, 1968.

Beer, G., *Die soziale und religiöse Stellung der Frau im israëlitischen Altertum*, Tübingen: Mohr, 1919.

Beard, M.R., *Woman as a Force in History: A Study in Traditions and Realities*, New York: Macmillan, 1946.

Bell, S.C. (ed.), *Women: From the Greeks to the French Revolution*, Belmont: Wadsworth, 1973.

Bird, P.A., '"Male and Female He created them": Gen. 1.27b in the Context of the Priestly Account of Creation', *HTR* 74 (1981), 129-159.

de Boer, P.A.H., *Fatherhood and Motherhood in Israelite and Judaite Piety*, Leiden: E.J. Brill, 1974.

Brenner, A., 'Naomi and Ruth', *VT* 33 (1983), 385-397.

Brooten, B.J., *Women Leaders in the Ancient Synagogue* (BJS, 36), Chico: Scholars Press, 1982.

Brown, F., Driver, S.R., Briggs, C.A., *A Hebrew and English Lexicon of the Old Testament*, Oxford: Clarendon Press, 1907 (= BDB).

Camp, C.V., 'The Wise Women of 2 Samuel: A Role Model for Women in Early Israel', *CBQ* 43 (1981), 14-29.

Campbell, E.F., 'The Hebrew Short Story: A Study of Ruth', *A Light unto My Path: Old Testament Studies in Honor of J.M. Myers* (ed. H.N. Bream *et al.*), Philadelphia: Temple University Press, 1974, 83-101.

Campbell, J., *The Hero with a Thousand Faces*, New York: Meridian, 1956.

Cassuto, U., 'Il palazzo di Baal', *Orientalia* 7 (1938), 266-286.

Childs, B.S., *Exodus* (OTL), London: SCM Press, 1968.

Clifford, R.J., 'Proverbs IX: A Suggested Ugaritic Parallel', *VT* 25 (1975), 298-306.

Coggins, R.J., *Ezra and Nehemiah* (CB), Cambridge: CUP, 1976.

Cohen, C. 'Widow', *Encyclopedia Judaica*, 1971, vol. 16, 487-495.

Cohen, S.J.D., 'Women in the Synagogues in Antiquity', *Conservative Judaism* 34 (1980), 23-29.

Craigie, P.C., 'The Song of Deborah and the Epic of Tukulti-Ninurta', *JBL* 87 (1969), 253-265.

Dundes, A. 'The Hero Pattern and the Life of Jesus', *Interpreting Folklore*, Bloomington: Indiana University Press, 1980, 223-261.

Eaubonne, F., *Les femmes avant la patriarchat*, Paris: Payot, 1976.

Eissfeldt, O. , *The Old Testament: An Introduction* (tr. P.R. Ackroyd), Oxford: Blackwell, 1966.

Emerton, J.A., 'Judah and Tamar', *VT* 29 (1969), 403-415.

Epstein, L.M., *Sex Laws and Customs in Judaism*, New York: Ktav, 1948/1967.

Ewart, A., *The World's Wickedest Women: Intriguing Studies of Eve and Evil through the Ages*, New York: Taplinger, 1964.

Falk, M., *Love Lyrics from the Bible*, Sheffield: Almond, 1983.

Fleming, W.B., *The History of Tyre*, New York: AMS Press, 1915/1966.

Fohrer, G., *Elia*, Zürich: Zwingli-Verlag, [2]1968.

Ford, P.J., 'Paul the Apostle: Male Chauvinist?', *BTB* 5 (1975), 303-311.

Gelb, I.J., Jacobson, T., Landsberger, B., Oppenheim, A.L., *The Assyrian Dictionary of the Oriental Institute of the University of Chicago*, Chicago: University of Chicago Press, 1956– (= CAD).

Ginsburg, C.D., *The Song of Songs and Coheleth*, New York: Ktav, 1857/1861/1970.

Goodwater, P., *Women in Antiquity: An Annotated Bibliography*, Metuchen, N.J.: Scarecrow Press, 1976.

Gordis, R., 'Love, Marriage, and Business in the Book of Ruth', *A Light unto My Path: Old Testament Studies in Honor of J.M. Myers* (ed. H.N. Bream *et al.*), Philadelphia: Temple University Press, 1974, 241-264.

Gray, J. *I and II Kings* (OTL), London: SCM Press, [3]1977.

Green, B., 'The Plot of the Biblical Story of Ruth', *JSOT* 23 (1982), 55-68.

Gruber, M., 'The Motherhood of God in Second Isaiah', *RB* 90 (1983), 351-359.

Gunkel, H., *Genesis*, Göttingen: Vandenhoeck und Ruprecht, [6]1964.

Hallo, W.W., 'Women of Sumer (Bibliotheca Mesopotamica IV, ed. Schamandt-Besserat D.), *The Legacy of Summer*, Austin: University of Texas Press, 1976.

Hanson, P.D., 'Masculine Metaphors of God and Sex Discrimination in the Old Testament', *Ecumenical Review* 4 (1975), 320-322.

Harris, R., 'The naditu Women', *Studies Presented to A. Leo Oppenheim*, Chicago: University of Chicago Press, 1964, 106-135.

Harter, L.B., 'The Theme of the Barren Woman in the Patriarchal Narratives', *Concern*, Nov. 1971, 20-24; Dec. 1971, 18-23.

Herodotus, *The Histories* (tr. A. de Sélincourt), Harmondsworth: Penguin, 1972/1975.

Hull, W.E., 'Woman in Her Place: Biblical Perspectives', *Review and*

Expositor, 72 (1975), 5-17.

Katzenstein, H.J.,—*The History of Tyre*, Jerusalem: Schocken Institute for Jewish Research, 1973.

—'Who Were the Parents of Athaliah?', *IEJ* 5 (1955), 194-197.

Landy, F., *Paradoxes of Paradise: Identity and Difference in the Song of Songs*, Sheffield: Almond, 1983.

Levenson, J.D., '1 Samuel 25 as Literature and as History', *CBQ* 40 (1978), 11-28.

Lewy, H., 'Nitroqris—Naqi'a', *JNES* 11 (1952), 264-286.

Liver, J.A.O., 'Deborah', *Encyclopedia Judaica*, 1971, vol. 5, 1429-1433.

Loewe, R., *The Position of Women in Judaism*, London: SPCK, 1966.

Malamat, A., 'Mari', *Encyclopedia Judaica*, 1971, vol. 11, 987-989.

McComisky, T.E., *The Status of the Secondary Wife: Its Development in Ancient Near Eastern Law*, Toronto: University Press, 1931.

McKane, W., *Proverbs* (OTL), London: SCM Press, 1970.

Meeks, W.A., 'The Image of the Androgyne', *History of Religion* 13 (1974), 165-208.

Michel, A. *et al.*, *Femmes, sexisme et sociétés*, Paris: Presses Universitaires de France, 1977.

Montgomery, J.A., and Gehman, H.S., *The Books of Kings* (ICC), Edinburgh: T. & T. Clark, 1951.

Murphy-O'Connor, J., 'Sex and Logic in 1 Cor. 2.2-16', *CBQ* 42 (1980), 482-499.

Noth, M., *Exodus* (OTL; tr. J.S. Bowden), London: SCM Press, 1962.

Nougier, L.R. *Histoire mondiale de la femme*, vol. 1: *Préhistoire et Antiquité* (ed. P. Grimal), Paris: Nouvelle Librairie de France, 1965.

Otwell, J.H., *And Sarah Laughed: The Status of Women in the Old Testament*, Philadelphia: Fortress Press, 1977.

Peritz, I.J., 'Women in the Ancient Hebrew Cult', *JBL* 17 (1898), 111-148.

Phillips, A., 'Some Aspects of Family Law in Pre-Exilic Israel', *VT* 23 (1973), 349-361.

Plaskow, J., and Romero, J.A. (eds.), *Women and Religion*, Missoula: Scholars Press, 1974.

Pomeroy, S.B., *Goddesses, Whores, Wives, and Slaves: Women in Classical Antiquity*, New York: Schocken, 1975.

Pope, M., *The Song of Songs* (AB), New York: Doubleday, 1977.

Pritchard, J.B., *Ancient New Eastern Texts Relating to the Old Testament*, Princeton: University Press, 1950 (= ANET).

Propp, V. *Morphology of the Folktale*, Austin: University of Texas Press, ²1968.

Rabin, C., 'The Song of Songs and Tamil Poetry', *Studies in Religion* 3 (1973), 205-219.

Raglan, F.R. Somerset, *The Hero: A Study in Tradition, Myth, and Drama*, New York: Vintage, 1936/1956.

Rank, O., *The Myth of the Birth of the Hero and Other Writings*, New York:

Vintage Books, 1959.

Ruether, R.R. (ed.), *Religion and Sexism: Images of Women in the Jewish and Christian Traditions*, New York: Simon and Schuster, 1974.

Sapp, S., *Sexuality, The Bible, and Science*, Philadelphia: Fortress Press, 1977.

Sasson, J.M., *Ruth*, Baltimore and London: Johns Hopkins, 1979.

Scott, R.B.Y., *Proverbs and Ecclesiastes* (AB), New York: Doubleday, 1965.

Scroggs, R.A.,—'Paul and the Eschatological Woman', *JAAR* 40 (1972), 283-303.

—'Paul and the Eschatological Woman: Revisited,' *JAAR* 42 (1974), 532-537.

Seltman, C.T., *Women in Antiquity*, New York: St Martin's Press, 1956.

Siddons, P.A., *A New Testament Perspective on the Quality of Women*, Colgate-Rochester Divinity School, 1980.

Stendahl, K., *The Bible and the Role of Women: A Case Study in Hermeneutics*, Philadelphia: Fortress Press, 1966.

Swidler, L., *Women in Judaism*, Metuchen, N.J.: Scarecrow Press, 1976.

Taylor, J.G., 'The Song of Deborah and Two Canaanite Goddesses', *JSOT* 23 (1982), 99-108.

Thackeray, H. St J., and Marcus, H. (eds.), *The Works of Josephus Flavius*, London: W. Heinemann, 1961-1965.

Thompson, R.C., *Semitic Magic: Its Origins and Development*, New York: AMS Press, 1976.

Trible, P., 'Depatriarchalizing in Biblical Interpretation', *JAAR* 41 (1973), 30-47.

—*God and the Rhetoric of Sexuality*, Philadelphia: Fortress Press, 1978.

—'Two Women in a Man's World: A Reading of the Book of Ruth', *Soundings* 49 (1976), 251-279.

Trompf, G.W., 'On Attitudes towards Women in Paul and Paulinist Literature: 1 Cor. 11:3-6 and Its Context', *CBQ* 42 (1980), 196-215.

Van Seters, J., 'The Problem of Childlessness in Near Eastern Law and the Patriarchs of Israel', *JBL* 87 (1968), 401-408.

Walker, W.O., '1 Cor. 11:2-16 and Paul's Views Regarding Women', *JBL* 94 (1975), 94-110.

Walsh, J.T., 'Gen. 2:4b–3:24: A Synchronic Approach', *JBL* 96 (1977), 161-177.

Weinfeld, M., *Deuteronomy and the Deuteronomic School*, Oxford: OUP, 1972.

Whybray, R.N., *The Book of Proverbs* (CB), Cambridge: CUP, 1972.

—*Wisdom in Proverbs*, London: SCM, 1965.

Williams, J.G., *Women Recounted: Narrative Thinking and the God of Israel*, Sheffield: Almond, 1982.

—'Yahweh, Women, and the Trinity', *Theology Today* 32 (1975), 234-242.

Zabriskie, C., 'A Psychological Analysis of Biblical Interpretations Pertaining to Women', *JPT* 4 (1976), 304–312.

Zimmerli, W., *Ezechiel 1–24* (BKAT 13/1), Neukirchen: Neukirchener Verlag, 1969.